Stephen Crane's
Battles

Stephen Crane's Battles

Nine Decisive Battles Recounted
by the Author of
The Red Badge of Courage

Stephen Crane

LEONAUR

Stephen Crane's Battles: Nine Decisive Battles
Recounted by the Author of *The Red Badge of Courage*
by Stephen Crane

Originally published under the title:
Great Battles of the World

Published by Leonaur Ltd

Copyright in this form © 2007 Leonaur Ltd

ISBN: 978-1-84677-209-2 (hardcover)
ISBN: 978-1-84677-210-8 (softcover)

http://www.leonaur.com

Contents

The Battle of Vittoria

AFTER THE FRENCH DEFEAT—VITTORIA

The Battle of Vittoria

The campaign of 1812, which included the storming of Ciudad Rodrigo and Badajoz and the overwhelming victory of Salamanca, had apparently done so much towards destroying the Napoleonic sway in the Peninsula that the defeat of the Allies at Burgos, in October 1812, came as an embittering disappointment to England; and when Wellington, after his disastrous retreat to Ciudad Rodrigo, reported his losses as amounting to nine thousand, the usual tempest of condemnation against him was raised, and the members of the Cabinet, who were always so free with their oracular advice and so close with the nation's money, wagged their heads despairingly.

But as the whole aspect of affairs was revealed, and as Wellington coolly stated his plans for a new campaign, public opinion changed.

It was a critical juncture: Napoleon had arranged an armistice with Russia, Prussia, and Austria, which was to last until August 16, 1813, and it became known that this armistice might end in peace. Peace on the Continent would mean that Napoleon's unemployed troops might be poured into Spain in such enormous numbers as to overwhelm the Allies. So, to ensure Wellington's striking a decisive blow before this could happen, both the English Ministry and the Opposition united in supporting him, and for the first time during the war he felt sure of receiving the supplies for which he had asked.

The winter and spring were spent by Wellington in preparing for his campaign: his troops needed severe discipline after the disorder into which they had fallen during the retreat from Burgos, and the great chief entered into the matter of their equipment with most painstaking attention to detail, removing unnecessary weight from them, and supplying each infantry soldier with three extra pairs of shoes, besides heels and soles for repairs. He drew large reinforcements from England, and all were drilled to a high state of efficiency.

It is well to quote here from the letter published by Wellington on the 28th of December 1812. It was addressed to the commanders of divisions and brigades. It created a very pretty storm, as one may readily see. I quote at length, since surely no document could be more illuminative of Wellington's character, and it seems certain that this fearless letter saved the army from the happy-go-lucky feeling, very common in British field forces, that a man is a thorough soldier so long as he is willing at all times to go into action and charge, if ordered, at even the brass gates of Inferno. But Wellington knew that this was not enough. He wrote as follows:

Gentlemen—I have ordered the army into cantonments, in which I hope that circumstances will enable me to keep them for some time, during which the troops will receive their clothing, necessaries, etc., which are already in progress by different lines of communication to the several divisions and brigades.

But besides these objects, I must draw your attention in a very particular manner to the state of discipline of the troops. The discipline of every army, after a long and active campaign, becomes in some degree relaxed, and requires the utmost attention on the part of general and other officers to bring it back to the state in which it ought to be for service; but I am concerned to have to observe that the army under my command has fallen off in this respect in the late campaign to a greater degree than any army with which I have ever served, or of which I have ever read.

It must be obvious, however, to every officer, that from the moment the troops commenced their retreat from the neighbourhood of Burgos on the one hand, and from Madrid on the other, the officers lost all command over their men.

I have no hesitation in attributing these evils to the habitual inattention of the officers of the regiments to their duty as prescribed by the standing regulations of the service and by the orders of this army.

I am far from questioning the zeal, still less the gallantry and spirit, of the officers of the army; I am quite certain that if their minds can be convinced of the necessity of minute and constant attention to understand, recollect, and carry into execution the orders which have been issued for the performance of their duty, and that the strict performance of this duty is necessary to enable the army to serve the country as it ought to be served, they will in future give their attention to these points.

Unfortunately, the experience of the officers of the army has induced many to consider that the period during which an army is on service is one of relaxation from all rule, instead of being, as it is, the period during which of all others every rule for the regulation and control of the conduct of the soldier, for the inspection and care of his arms, ammunition, accoutrements, necessaries, and field equipments, and his horse and horse appointments, for the receipt and issue and care of his provisions and the regulation of all that belongs to his food and the forage for his horse, must be most strictly attended to by the officer of his company or troop, if it is intended that an army—a British army in particular—shall be brought into the field of battle in a state of efficiency to meet the enemy on the day of trial.

These are points, then, to which I most earnestly entreat you to turn your attention, and the attention of the officers of the regiments under your command, Portuguese as well as English, during the period in which it may be in my power to leave the troops in their cantonments.

In regard to the food of the soldier, I have frequently observed and lamented in the late campaign the facility and celerity with which the French soldiers cooked in comparison with those of our army.

The cause of this disadvantage is the same with that of every other description—the want of attention of the officers to the orders of the army and the conduct of their men, and the consequent want of authority over their conduct.

But I repeat that the great object of the attention of the general and field officers must be to get the captains and subalterns of the regiments to understand and perform the duties required from them, as the only mode by which the discipline and efficiency of the army can be restored and maintained during the next campaign.

The British general never refrained from speaking his mind, even if his ideas were certain to be contrary to the spirit of the army. I will quote from Victories of The British Armies as follows:

Colborne marched with the infantry on the right; Head, with the Thirteenth Light Dragoons and two squadrons of Portuguese, on the left, and the heavy cavalry formed a reserve. Perceiving that their battering train was endangered, the French cavalry, as the ground over which they were retiring was favourable for the movement, charged the Thirteenth. But they were vigorously repulsed; and, failing in breaking the British, the whole, consisting of four regiments, drew up in front, forming an imposing line. The Thirteenth instantly formed and galloped forward—and nothing could have been more splendid than their charge. They rode fairly through the French, overtook and cut down many of the gunners, and at last entirely headed the line of march, keeping. up a fierce and straggling encounter with the broken horsemen of the enemy, until some of the English dragoons actually reached the gates of Badajoz.

And now I quote from Wellington's comment to Colborne:

I wish you would call together the officers of the dragoons and point out to them the mischiefs which must result from the disorder of the troops in action. The undisciplined ardour of the Thirteenth Dragoons and First Regiment of Portuguese cavalry is not of the description of the determined bravery and steadiness of soldiers confident in their discipline and in their officers. Their conduct was that of a rabble, galloping as fast as their horses could carry them over a plain, after an enemy to whom they could do no mischief when they were broken and the pursuit had continued for a limited distance, and sacrificing substantial advantages and all the objects of your operation by their want of discipline. To this description of their conduct I add my entire conviction, that if the enemy could have thrown out of Badajoz only one hundred men regularly formed, they would have driven back these two regiments in equal haste and disorder, and would probably have taken many whose horses would have been knocked up. If the Thirteenth Dragoons are again guilty of this conduct I shall take their horses from them, and send the officers and men to do duty at Lisbon.

The incident of the dragoons' charge happened early in 1811, but it shows how Wellington dealt with the firebrands in the army. However, imagine the feelings of the Thirteenth Dragoons!

As for the Allies, they were for a long time considered quite hopeless by British officers; the Portuguese were commonly known in the ranks as the *Vamosses*, from *vamos,* "let us be off," which they shouted before they ran away. (The American slang *vamoose* may have had its origin in the Mexican War.)

The Spanish and Portuguese hated each other so cordially that it was with the greatest difficulty that they could be induced to co-operate: they were continually plotting to betray each other, and, incidentally, the English. Wellington had a sufficiently hard task in keeping his English army in order and directing the civil administration of Portugal, which would otherwise have tumbled to pieces from the corruption of its government; but hardest of all was the military training of the Spanish and Portuguese. He was now in supreme command of the Spanish army, concerning which he had written:

> There is not in the whole Kingdom of Spain a depot of provisions for the support of a single battalion in operation for one day. Not a shilling of money in any military chest. To move them forward at any point now would be to ensure their certain destruction.

After that was written, however, he had been able to equip them with some degree of effectiveness, and had worked them up to a certain standard of discipline: they were brave and patient, and susceptible to improvement under systematic training. Beresford had also accomplished wonders with the Portuguese, and Wellington's army now numbered seventy thousand men, of whom forty thousand were British.

Wellington, with his lean, sharp-featured face, and dry, cold manner, was not the typical Englishman at all. He was more like the genuine Yankee of New England. He made his successes by his resourcefulness, his inability to be overpowered by circumstances. As he said:

> The French plan their campaigns just as you might make a splendid set of harness. It answers very well until

it gets broken, and then you are done for! Now I made my campaign of ropes; if anything went wrong I tied a knot and went on.

He was always ready, when anything broke or failed him, to "tie a knot and go on." That is the suppleness and adroitness of a great chieftain, whereas the typical English general was too magnificent for the little things; he liked to hurl his men boldly into the abyss—and then, if they perished, it had been magnificently done, at any rate. But Wellington was always practical and ready to take advantage of any opportunity that offered. He had no illusions about the grandeur of getting men killed for nothing.

There were still two hundred and thirty thousand French troops in Spain, but they were scattered across the Peninsula from Asturias to Valencia. To the extreme east was Marshal Suchet with sixty-five thousand men, and an expedition under General Murray was sent against him which kept him there. Clausel was prevented from leaving Biscay with his forty thousand men by the great guerrilla warfare with which Wellington enveloped his forces. There remained, then, for Wellington to deal with the centre of the army under Joseph Bonaparte, whose jealous suspicions had been the means of driving from Spain Marshal Soult, a really fine and capable commander. The weak Joseph was now the head of an immense and magnificently equipped army of men and officers in the finest condition for fighting, but who were to prove of how little effect fine soldiers can be when they lack the right chief.

The army of Joseph lay in a curve from Toledo to Zamora, guarding the central valley of the Douro, and covering the great road from Madrid through Burgos and Vittoria to France. Wellington's plan was to move the left wing of his army across the Douro within the Portuguese frontier, to march it up the right bank of the Douro as far as Zamora, and then, crossing the Elsa, to unite it to the Galician forces; while the centre and right, advancing from Agueda by Salamanca, were to force the passage of the Tormes and drive the French entirely from the line of the Douro towards the Carrion.

By constantly threatening them on the flank with the left wing, which was. to be always kept in advance, he thus hoped to drive the French back by Burgos into Biscay. He himself expected to establish there a new basis for the war among the numerous and well-fortified seaports on the coast. In this way, forcing the enemy back to his frontier, he would at once better his own position and intercept the whole communication of the enemy. The plan had the obvious objection that in separating his army into two forces, with great mountain ranges and impassable rivers between them, each was exposed to the risk of an attack by the whole force of the enemy.

But Wellington had resolved to take this risk. Sir Thomas Graham, in spite of his sixty-eight years, had the vigour and clear-headedness of youth, and the very genius for the difficult command given him—that of leading the left wing through virgin forests, over rugged mountains, and across deep rivers.

The march of Wellington began May 22, and an exalted spirit of enthusiasm pervaded the entire army. Even Wellington became expressive, and as he passed the stream that marks the frontier of Spain he arose in his stirrups, and, waving his hand, exclaimed, "Farewell, Portugal!"

Meanwhile Graham, on May 16, with forty thousand men, had crossed the Douro and pushed ahead, turning the French right and striking at their communications. Within ten days forty thousand men were transported through two hundred miles of the most broken and rugged country in the Peninsula, with all their artillery and baggage. Soon they were in possession of the whole crest of mountains between the Ebro and the sea. On the 31st Graham reached the Elsa. The French were astounded when Graham appeared upon their flank; they abandoned their strong position on the Douro; then they abandoned Madrid; after that, they hurried out of Burgos and Valladolid.

Wellington had crossed the Douro at Miranda on May 25, in advance of his troops, by means of a basket slung on a rope from precipice to precipice, at an immense height above the foaming torrent. The rivers were all swollen by floods.

Graham, with the left wing of the Allies, kept up his eager march. Many men were lost while fording the Elsa on May 31. The water was almost chin-deep and the bottom was covered with shifting stones. Graham hastened with fierce speed to the Ebro, eager to cross it before Joseph and break his communications with France. Joseph had wished to stop his retreat at Burgos and give battle there, but he had been told that incredible numbers of guerrillas had joined the English forces, and so he pushed on, leaving the castle at Burgos heavily mined. It was calculated that the explosion would take place just as the English entered the town, but the fuses were too quick—three thousand French soldiers, the last to leave, were crushed by the falling ruins. The allied troops marched triumphantly through the scene of their earlier struggle and defeat.

On abandoning Burgos Joseph took the road to Vittoria and sent pressing orders to Clausel to join him there, but this junction of forces was not effected—Clausel was too late.

Wellington's strategy of turning the French right has been called "the most masterly movement made during the Peninsular War." Its chief merit was that it gave Wellington the advantage of victory with hardly any loss of life. It swept the French back to the Spanish frontier. And Joseph, whose train comprised an incredible number of chariots, carriages, and wagons, bearing a helpless multitude of people of both sexes from Madrid (including the civil functionaries and officers of his court), as well as enormous stores of spoil, began to perceive that this precipitate retreat was his ruin, and that he must risk the chance of a great battle to escape being driven in hopeless confusion through the passes of the Pyrenees.

The sweep of the Allies under Graham around the French right had taken them through the wildest and most enchantingly beautiful regions. At times a hundred men had been needed to drag up one piece of artillery. Again, the guns would be lowered down a precipice by ropes, or forced up the rugged goat-paths. At length, to quote Napier, "the scarlet uniforms were to be seen in every valley, and the stream of war, descending with impetuous force down all the clefts of the mountains, burst in a hundred foaming torrents into the basin of Vittoria."

So accurately had Graham done his work in accordance with Wellington's plans, that he reached the valley just as Joseph's dejected troops were forming themselves in front of Vittoria.

The basin or valley of Vittoria, with the town in its eastern extremity, is a small plain about eight miles by six miles in extent, situated in an elevated plateau among the mountains and guarded on all sides by rugged hills.

The great road from Madrid enters the valley at the Puebla Pass, where too the river Zadora flows through a narrow mountain gorge. This road then runs up the left bank of the Zadora to Vittoria, and from there it goes on towards Bayonne and the Pyrenees. This road was Joseph's line of retreat.

King Joseph, burdened by his treasure, which included the plunder of five years of French occupation in the Peninsula, and consisted largely of priceless works of art, selected with most excellent taste by himself and other French connoisseurs, had despatched to France two great convoys, a small part of the whole treasure, along the Bayonne road. As these had to be heavily guarded against the Biscay guerrillas, some thousands of troops had gone with them. Joseph's remaining forces were estimated at from sixty thousand to sixty-five thousand men.

The French were anxious above all things to keep the road open—the road to Bayonne: there are several rough mountain roads intersecting each other at Vittoria, particularly those to Pampeluna, Bilboa, and Galicia; but the great Bayonne road was the only one capable of receiving the huge train of lumbering carriages without which the army was not to move.

On the afternoon of the 20th Wellington, whose effective force was now sixty-five thousand men, surveyed the place and the enemy from the hill ranges and saw that they were making a stand. He decided then on his tactics. Instead of pushing on his combined forces to a frontal attack, he made up his mind to divide his troops; he would send Graham with the left wing, consisting of eighteen thousand men and twenty guns, around by the northern hills to the rear of the French army, there to seize the road to Bayonne. Sir Rowland Hill with twenty thousand men, including General Murillo with his Spaniards, was to move with the right wing, break through the Puebla Pass, and attack the French left.

The right centre under Wellington himself was to cross the ridges forming the southern boundary of the basin and then move straight forward to the Zadora River and attack the bridges, while the left centre was to move across the bridge of Mendoza in the direction of the town.

The French right, which Graham was to attack, occupied the heights in front of the Zadora River above the village of Abechucho, and covered Vittoria from approach by the Bilboa road; the centre extended along the left bank of the Zadora, commanding the bridges in front of it, and blocking up the great road from Madrid. The left occupied the space from Ariniz to the ridges of Puebla de Arlauzon, and guarded the Pass of Puebla, by which Hill was to enter the valley.

The early morning of June 21 was, according to one historian, " rainy and heavy with vapour," while an observer (Leith Hay) said: "The morning was extremely brilliant; a clearer or more beautiful atmosphere never favoured the progress of a gigantic conflict."

The valley, occupied by the French army, with the rich uniforms of its officers, was a superb spectacle. Marshal Jourdan, the commander, could be seen riding slowly along the line of his troops. The positions they occupied rose in steps from the centre of the valley, so that all could be seen by the English from the crest of the Morillas as they stood ready for battle. In his *Events of Military Life* Henry says:

> The dark and formidable masses of the French were prepared at all points to repel the meditated attack—the infantry in column with loaded arms, or ambushed thickly in the low woods at the base of their position, the cavalry in lines with drawn swords, and the artillery frowning from the eminences with lighted matches; while on our side all was yet quietness and repose. The chiefs were making their observations, and the men walking about in groups amidst the piled arms, chatting and laughing and gazing, and apparently not caring a pin for the fierce hostile array in their front.

At ten o'clock Hill reached the Pass of Puebla and forced his way through with extraordinary swiftness. Murillo's Spaniards went swarming up the steep ridges to dislodge the French, but the enemy made a furious resistance, and reinforcements kept coming to their aid. General Murillo was wounded, but would not be carried from the field. Hill then sent the Seventy-first to help the Spaniards, who were showing high courage, but being terribly mown down by the French musketry.

Colonel Cadogan, who led the Seventy-first, had no sooner reached the summit of the height than he fell, mortally wounded. The French were driven from their position, but the loss of Cadogan was keenly felt. The story of his strange state of exaltation the night before the battle is well known—his rapture at the prospect of taking part in it. As he lay dying on the summit he would not be moved, although the dead lay thick about him, but watched the progress of his Highlanders until he could no longer see.

While this conflict was going on, Wellington, with the right centre, had commenced his attack on the bridges over the Zadora. A Spanish peasant brought word that the bridge of Tres Puentes was negligently guarded, and offered to guide the troops to it. Kempt's Brigade soon reached it; the Fifteenth Hussars galloped over, but a shot from a French battery killed the brave peasant who had guided them.

The forces that crossed at Tres Puentes now formed under the shelter of a hill. One of the officers wrote of this position:

> Our post was most extraordinary, as we were isolated from the rest of the army and within one hundred yards of the enemy's advance. As I looked over the bank, I could see El Rey Joseph, surrounded by at least five thousand men, within five hundred yards of us.

It has always seemed an inconceivable thing that the French should not have destroyed the seven narrow bridges across the Zadora before the 21st had dawned. Whether it was from over-confidence or sheer mental confusion, it is impossible to know.

The Third and Seventh Divisions were now moving rapidly down to the bridge of Mendoza, but the enemy's light troops and guns had opened a vigorous fire upon them, until the riflemen of the Light Division, who had crossed at Tres Puentes, charged the enemy's fire, and the bridge was carried.

Sir Thomas Picton was a picturesque figure in this part of the operations. Through some oversight he and his men, the " Fighting Third," were neglected. Orders came to other troops, bridges were being carried, but no word was sent to Picton. "D— it!" he cried out to one of his officers, "Lord Wellington must have forgotten us!" He beat the mane of his horse with his stick in his impatience and anger. Finally, an aide-de-camp galloped up and inquired for Lord Dalhousie, who commanded the Seventh Division. In answer to Picton's inquiries he stated that he brought orders for Dalhousie to carry the bridge to the left, while the Fourth and Sixth Divisions were to support the attack. Picton rose in his stirrups, and shouted angrily to the amazed aide-de-camp:

"You may tell Lord Wellington from me, sir, that the Third Division, under my command, shall in less than ten minutes attack the bridge and carry it, and the Fourth and Sixth may support if they choose." Then, addressing his men with his customary blend of affection and profanity, he cried: "Come on, ye rascals! Come on, ye fighting villains!"

They carried the bridge with such fire and speed that the whole British line was animated by the sight.

Maxwell says:

> The passage of the river, the movement of glittering masses from right to left as far as the eye could range, the deafening roar of cannon, the sustained fusillade of the artillery, made up a magnificent scene. The British cavalry, drawn up to support the columns, seemed a glittering line of golden helmets and sparkling swords in the keen sunshine which now shone upon the field of battle.

L'Estrange, who was with the Thirty-first, says that the men were marching through standing corn (I suppose some kind of grain that ripens early, certainly not maize) yellow for the sickle and between four and five feet high, and the hissing cannon-balls, as they rent their way through the sea of golden grain, made long furrows in it.

The hill in front of Ariniz was the key of the French line, and Wellington brought up several batteries and hurled Picton's division in a solid mass against it, while the heavy cavalry of the British came up at a gallop from the river to sustain the attack.

This hill had been the scene of a great fight in the wars of the Black Prince, where Sir William Felton, with two hundred archers and swordsmen, had been surrounded by six thousand Spaniards, and all perished, resisting doggedly. It is still called "the Englishmen's hill."

An obstinate fight now raged, for a brief space, on this

spot. A long wall was held by several battalions of French infantry, whose fire was so deadly as to check the British for a time. They reached the wall, however, and for a few moments on either side of it was a seething mass of furious soldiers. "Any person," said Kincaid, who was present, "who chose to put his head over from either side, was sure of getting a sword or bayonet up his nostrils."

As the British broke over the wall, the French. fell back, abandoning Ariniz for the ridge in front of Gomecha, only to be forced back again.

It was the noise of Graham's guns, booming since mid-day at their rear, that took the heart out of the French soldiery.

Graham had struck the great blow on the left; at eleven he had reached the heights above the village and bridge of Gamara Major, which were strongly occupied by the French under Reille. General Oswald commenced the attack and drove the enemy from the heights; then Major-General Robinson, at the head of a brigade of the Fifth Division, formed his men and led them forward on the run to carry the bridge and village of Gamara. But the French fire was so strong that he was compelled to fall back. Again he rallied them and crossed the bridge, but the French drove them back once more. Fresh British troops came up and the bridge was carried again; and then, for the third time, it was lost under Reille's murderous fire.

But now the panic from the centre had reached Reille. It was known that the French centre was retreating: the Frenchmen had no longer the moral strength to resist Robinson's attacks, and so the bridge was won by the English and the Bayonne road was lost to the French.

In the centre the battle had become a sort of running fight for six miles; the French were at last all thrown back into the little plain in front of Vittoria, where from the crowded throng cries of despair could be heard.

"At six o'clock," Maxwell says, "the sun was setting, and his last rays fell upon a dreadful spectacle: red masses of infantry were advancing steadily across the plain; the horse artillery came at a gallop to the front to open its fire upon the fugitives; the Hussar Brigade was charging by the Camino Real."

Of the helpless encumbrances of the French army an eyewitness said:

> Behind them was the plain in which the city stood, and beyond the city thousands of carriages and animals and non-combatants, men, women, and children, were crowding together in all the madness of terror; and as the English shot went booming overhead the vast crowd started and swerved with a convulsive movement, while a dull and horrid sound of distress arose.

Joseph now ordered the retreat to be conducted by the only road left open—that to Pampeluna, but it was impossible to take away his train of carriages. He, the king, only escaped capture by jumping out of one door of his carriage as his pursuers reached the other: he left his sword of state in it, and the beautiful Correggio " Christ in the Garden," now at Apsley House, in England.

Eighty pieces of cannon, jammed close together near Vittoria on the only remaining defensible ridge near the town, had kept up a desperate fire to the last, and Reille had held his ground near the Zadora heroically, but it was useless. The great road to Bayonne was lost, and finally that to Pampeluna was choked with broken-down carriages. The British dragoons were pursuing hotly, and the frantic French soldiers plunged into morasses, over fields and hills, in the wildest rout, leaving their artillery, ammunition-wagons, and the spoil of a kingdom.

The outskirts of Vittoria were strewn with the wreckage. Never before in modern times had such a quantity of spoil fallen into the hands of a victorious army. There were objects of interest from museums, convents, and royal palaces; there were jewels of royal worth and masterpieces of Titian, Raphael, and Correggio.

The marshal's baton belonging to Jourdan had been left, with one hundred and fifty-one brass guns, four hundred and fifteen caissons of ammunition, one million three hundred thousand ball cartridges, fourteen thousand rounds of artillery ammunition, and forty thousand pounds of gunpowder. Joseph's power was gone: he was only a wretched fugitive. Six thousand of his men had been killed and wounded, and one thousand were prisoners.

It has not been possible to estimate the value of the private plunder, but five and a-half millions of dollars in the military chest of the army were taken, and untold quantities of private wealth were also lost to their owners; it was all scattered— shining heaps of gold and silver—over the road, and the British soldiers reaped it. Wellington refused to make any effort to induce his men to give up the enormous sums they had absorbed: "They have earned it," he said. But he had reason to regret it. They fell into frightful orgies of intemperance that lasted for days. Wellington wrote Lord Bathurst, June 29:

> We started with the army in the highest order, and up to the day of the battle nothing could get on better. But that event has, as usual, totally annihilated all order and discipline. The soldiers of the army have got among them about a million sterling in money, with the exception of about one hundred thousand dollars which were got in the military chest. I am convinced that we have now out of our ranks double the amount of our loss in the battle, and have lost more men in the pursuit than the enemy have.

It was calculated that seven thousand five hundred men had straggled from the effects of the plunder.

The convoys sent ahead by Joseph had contained some of the choicest works of art; they reached France safely, and are displayed in the museums of Paris. In justice to the Duke of Wellington it must be said that he communicated with Ferdinand, offering to restore the paintings which had fallen into his hands, but Ferdinand desired him to keep them. The wives of the French officers were sent on to Pampeluna the next day by Wellington, who had treated them with great kindness.

As for the rest of the feminine army, the nuns, the actresses, and the superbly arrayed others, they made their escape with greater difficulties and hardships. Alison says:

> Rich vestures of all sorts, velvet and silk brocades, gold and silver plate, noble pictures, jewels, laces, cases of claret and champagne, poodles, parrots, monkeys, and trinkets lay scattered about the fields in endless confusion, amidst weeping mothers, wailing infants, and all the unutterable miseries of warlike overthrow.

Napoleon was filled with fury at his brother for the result of Vittoria, but he instructed his ministers to say that "a somewhat brisk engagement with the English took place at Vittoria in which both sides lost equally. The French armies, however, carried out the movements in which they were engaged, but the enemy seized about one hundred guns which were left without teams at Vittoria, and it is these that the English are trying to pass off as artillery captured on the battlefield!"

One of the most important captures of the battle was a mass of documents from the archives of Madrid, including a great part of Napoleon's secret correspondence—an invaluable addition to history.

Napier's summing up of the results of the battle reads:

> Joseph's reign was over; the crown had fallen from his head. And, after years of toils and combats, which had been rather admired than understood, the English general, emerging from the chaos of the Peninsula struggle, stood on the summit of the Pyrenees a recognised conqueror. From these lofty pinnacles

the clangour of his trumpets pealed clear and loud, and the splendour of his genius appeared as a flaming beacon to warring nations.

However, Napier always was inclined to be eloquent. Perhaps it was lucky for Wellington that the worthless make-trouble, Joseph Bonaparte, had been in the place of his tremendous brother.

The Siege of Plevna

OSMAN PASHA IN THE SORTIE FROM PLEVNA

The Siege of Plevna

When the Russian army swarmed through the Shipka Pass of the Balkans there was really nothing before it but a man and an opportunity. Osman Pasha suddenly and with great dexterity took his force into Plevna, a small Bulgarian town near the Russian line of march.

The military importance of Plevna lay in the fact that this mere village of seventeen hundred people was the junction of the roads from Widin, Sophia, Biela, Zimnitza, Nikopolis, and the Shipka Pass. Osman's move was almost entirely on his own initiative. He had no great reputation, and, like Wellington in the early part of the Peninsula campaign, he was obliged to do everything with the strength of his own shoulders. The stupidity of his superiors amounted almost to an oppression.

The Russians recognised the strategic importance of Plevna a moment too late. On July 18, 1877, General Krudener at Nikopolis received orders to occupy Plevna at once. He seems to have moved promptly, but long before he could arrive Osman's tired but dogged battalions were already in the position.

The Turkish regular of that day must have resembled very closely his fellow of the present. Von Moltke, who knew the Turks well, and whose remarkable mind clearly outlined and prophesied the result of several more recent Balkan campaigns, said, "An impetuous attack may be expected from the Turks, but not an obstinate and lasting defence." Historically, the opinion of the great German field-marshal seems very curious. Even in the late war between Greece and Turkey the attacks of the Turkish troops were usually anything but impetuous. They were fearless, but very leisurely. As to the lasting and obstinate defence, one has only to regard the siege of Plevna to understand that Von Moltke was for the moment writing carelessly.

After Plevna, the word went forth that the most valuable weapon of the Turk was his shovel. When Osman arrived, the defences of Plevna consisted of an ordinary block-house, but he at once set his troops at work digging entrenchments and throwing up redoubts, which were located with great skill. Soon the vicinity of the town was one great fortress. Osman coolly was attempting to stem the Russian invasion with a force of these strange Turkish troops, patient, enduring, sweet-tempered, and ignorant, dressed in slovenly overcoats and sheep-skin sandals, living on a diet of black bread and cucumbers.

Receiving the order from the Grand Duke Nicolas, General Krudener at Nikopolis despatched at dawn of the next day six thousand five hundred men, with about seven batteries, to Plevna. No effective scouting had been done. The Russian general, Schilder-Schuldner, riding comfortably in his carriage in the customary way of Russian commanders of the time, had absolutely no information that a strong Turkish force had occupied the position. His column had been allowed to distribute itself over a distance of seventeen miles. On the morning of the 20th an attack was made with great confidence by the troops which had come up. Two Russian regiments even marched victoriously through the streets of Plevna, throwing down their heavy packs and singing for joy of the easy capture. But suddenly a frightful fusillade began from all sides. The elated regiments melted in the streets. Infuriated by religious ardour, despising the value of a Christian's life, the Turks poured out from their concealed places, and there occurred a great butchery. The Russian Nineteenth Regiment of the line was cut down to a few fragments. Much artillery ammunition was captured. The Russians lost two thousand seven hundred men. The knives of the Circassians and Bashi-Bazouks had been busy in the streets.

After this victory Osman might have whipped Krudener, but the Russian leaders had been suddenly aroused to the importance of taking Plevna, and Krudener was almost immediately reinforced with three divisions. Within the circle of defence the Turk was using his shovel. Osman gave the garrison no rest. If a man was not shooting, he was digging. The well-known Grivitza Redoubt was greatly strengthened, and some defences on the east side of the town were completed. Osman's situation was desperate, but his duty to his country was vividly defined. If he could hold this strong Turkish, force on the flank of the Russians, their advance on Constantinople would hardly be possible. The Russian leaders now thoroughly understood this fact, and they tried to make the army investing Plevna more than a containing force.

The Grand Duke Nicolas had decided to order an assault on the 30th of July. Krudener telegraphed—the grand duke was thirty miles from Plevna—that he hesitated in his views of prospective success. The grand duke replied sharply, ordering that the assault be made. It seems that Krudener went into the field in the full expectation of being beaten.

Now appears in the history of the siege a figure at once sinister and foolish. Subordinate in command to Krudener was Lieutenant-General Prince Schahofskoy, who had an acute sense of his own intelligence, and in most cases dared to act independently of the orders of his chief. But to offset him there suddenly galloped into his camp a brilliant young Russian commander, a man who has set his name upon Plevna, even as, the word underlies the towering reputation of Osman Pasha. General Skobeleff had come from the Grand

Duke Nicolas with an order directing Prince Schahofskoy to place the young man in command of a certain brigade of Caucasian Cossacks. The prince grew stormy with outraged pride, and practically told Skobeleff to take the Cossacks and go to the devil with them.

The Russians began a heavy bombardment, to which Osman's guns replied with spirit. The key of the position was the Grivitza Redoubt. Krudener himself attacked it with eighteen battalions of infantry and ten batteries. And at the same time Prince Schahofskoy thundered away on his side. The latter at last became furious at Krudener's lack of success, and resolved to take matters into his own hands. In the afternoon he advanced with three brigades in the face of a devastating Turkish fire, took a hill, and forced the Turks to vacate their first line of entrenchments. His men were completely spent with weariness, and it is supposed that he should have waited on the hill for support from Krudener. But he urged on his tired troops and carried a second position. The Turkish batteries now concentrated their fire upon his line, and, really, the Turkish infantry whipped him soundly.

The Russians did not give up the dearly bought gain of ground without desperate fighting. Again and again they furiously charged, but only to meet failure. When night fell, the stealthy-footed irregular of the Turkish forces crept through the darkness to prey upon the route of the Russian retreat. The utter annihilation of Prince Schahofskoy's force was prevented by Skobeleff and the brigade of Cossacks with which the prince had sent him to the devil. Skobeleff's part in this assault was really a matter of clever manoeuvring.

Krudener had failed with gallantry and intelligence. Schahofskoy had failed through pigheadedness and self-confidence.

After this attempt to carry Plevna, the important Russian generals occupied themselves in mutual recriminations. Krudener bitterly blamed Schahofskoy for not obeying his orders, and Schahofskoy acidulously begged to know why

Krudener had not supported him. At the same time they both claimed that the Grand Duke Nicolas, thirty miles away, should never have given an order for an assault on a position of which he had never had a view.

But even if Russian clothing and arms and trinkets were being sold for a pittance in the bazaars of Plevna, the mosques were jammed with wounded Turks, and such was the suffering that the dead in the streets and in the fields were being gnawed by the pervasive Turkish dog.

A few days later Osman Pasha received the first proper recognition from Constantinople. A small troop of cavalry had wormed its way into Plevna. It was headed by an aide-de-camp of the Sultan. In gorgeous uniform the aide appeared to Osman and presented him with the First Order of the Os-manli, the highest Turkish military decoration. And with this order came a sword, the hilt of which flamed with diamonds. Osman Pasha may have preferred a bushel of cucumbers, but at any rate he knew that the Sultan and Turkey at last understood the value of a good soldier. To the speech of the aide Osman replied with another little speech, and the soldiers in their entrenchments cheered the Sultan.

On August 31 the Turkish general made his one offensive move. He threw part of his force against a Russian redoubt and was obliged to retire with a loss of nearly three thousand men. Afterwards he devoted his troops mainly to the business of improving the defences. He wasted no more in attempts to break out of Plevna.

At this late day of the siege, Prince Charles of Romania was appointed to the chief command of the whole Russo-Rumanian army. But naturally this office was nominal. General Totoff had the real disposition of affairs, but he did not hold it very long. General Levitsky, the assistant chief of the Russian general staff, arrived do advise General Totoff under direct orders from the Grand Duke Nicolas. But this siege was to be very well generalled.

The Grand Duke Nicolas himself came to Plevna. One would think that the grand duke would have ended this kaleidoscopic row of superseding generals. But the Great White Czar himself appeared. Osman Pasha, shut up in Plevna, certainly was honoured with a great deal of distinguished interest.

However, Alexander II. did his best to give no orders. He had no illusions concerning his military knowledge. With a spirit profoundly kind and gentle, he simply prayed that no more lives would be lost. It is difficult to think what he had to say to his multitudinous generals, each of whom was the genius of the only true plan for capturing Plevna.

At daylight on the 7th of September the Turks saw that the entire army of the enemy had closed in upon them. Amid fields of ripening grain shone the smart red jackets of the hussars. The Turks saw the Bulgarians in sheepskin caps, and with their broad scarlet sashes stuck full of knives and pistols. They saw the queer round oilskin shakoes of the Cossacks and the greatcoats of thick grey blanketing. They saw the uniforms of the Russian infantry, the green tunics striped with red. For five days the smoke lay heavy over Plevna.

The 11th was the fete-day of the emperor, and the general assault on that day was arranged as if it had been part of a fete. The cannonade was to begin at daybreak along the whole line and stop at eight o'clock in the morning. The artillery was to play again from eleven o'clock until one o'clock. Then it was to play again from half-past two o'clock to three o'clock.

Directly afterwards the Rumanian allies of the Russians moved in three columns against the Grivitza Redoubt. At first all three were repulsed, but with the stimulus of Russian reinforcements they rallied, and after a long time of almost hand-to-hand fighting the evening closed with them in possession of what was called the key of the Plevna position. They had lost four thousand men. The victory was fruitless, as, anticipating the attack on Grivitza, Osman had caused the building of an inner redoubt. After all their ferocious charging, the Russians were really no nearer to success.

At three o'clock of that afternoon Redoubt Number Ten had been assailed by General Schmidnikoff. The firing had been terrible, but the Russians had charged to the very walls of the redoubt. The Turks not only beat them off, but pursued with great spirit. Two of the scampering Russian battalions were then faced about to beat off the chase. They lay down at a distance of only two hundred yards of the redoubt, and sent the Turks pell-mell back into their fortifications.

At about the same time Skobeleff, wearing a white coat and mounted on a white charger, was leading his men over the "green hills" towards the Krishin Redoubt. There was a dense fog. Skobeleff's troops crossed two ridges and waded a stream. They began the ascent of a steep slope. Suddenly the fog cleared; the sun shone out brilliantly. The closely massed Russian force was exposed at range to line after line of Turkish entrenchments. They retired once, but rallied splendidly, and before five o'clock Skobeleff found himself in possession of Redoubt Number Eleven and Redoubt Number Twelve.

His battalions were thrust like a wedge into the Turkish lines, but the Turkish commander appreciated the situation more clearly than any Russian save Skobeleff. The latter's men suffered a frightful fire. Reinforcements were refused. All during the night the faithful troops of the czar fought in darkness and without hope. They even built little ramparts of dead men. But on the morning of September 12 Skobeleff was compelled to give up all he had gained. The retreat over the "green hills" was little more than a running massacre.

After his return Skobeleff was in a state of excitement and fury. His uniform was covered with blood and mud. His Cross of St. George was twisted around over his shoulder. His face was black with powder. His eyes were bloodshot. He said, "My regiments no longer exist."

The Russian assaults had failed at all points. They had

begun this last battle with thirty thousand infantry, twelve thousand cavalry, and four hundred and forty guns, and they lost over eighteen thousand men. The multitude of generals again took counsel. There were fervid animosities, and there might have been open rupture if it were not for the presence of the czar himself, whose gentleness and good nature prevented many scenes.

It was decided that the Turks must be starved out. The Russians sent for more troops as well as for heavy supplies of clothing, ammunition, and food. The czar sent for General Todleben, who had shown great skill at Sebastopol, and the direction of the siege was put in his hands.

The Turks had been accustomed to reprovision Plevna by the skilful use of devious trails. Todleben took swift steps to put a stop to it, but he did not succeed before a huge convoy had been sent into the town through the adroit management of Chefket Pasha. But the Russian horse soon chased Chefket away, and the trails were all closed.

For the most part the September weather was fine, but this plenitude of sun made the Turkish positions about Plevna almost unbearable. Actual thousands of unburied dead lay scattered over the ridges. At one time the Russian headquarters made a polite request to be allowed to send some men to enter Grivitza and bury their own dead. But this polite request met with polite refusal.

On October 19 the Rumanians, who for weeks had been sapping their way up to the Grivitza Redoubt, made a final and desperate attack on it. They were repulsed.

In order to complete the investment, Todleben found it necessary to dislodge the Turks from four villages near Plevna.

The weeks moved by slowly with a stolid and stubborn Turk besieged by.^ stubborn and stolid Russian. There was occasional firing from the Russian batteries, to which the Turks did not always take occasion to reply. In Plevna there was nothing to eat but meat, and the Turkish soldiers moved about with the hoods of their dirty brown cloaks pulled over their heads. Outside Plevna there were plenty of furs and good coats, but the diet had become so plain that the sugar-loving Russian soldiers would give gold for a pot of jam.

On the cold, cloudy morning of December 11, when snow lay thickly on all the country, a sudden great booming of guns was heard, and the news flew swiftly that Osman had come out of Plevna at last, and was trying to break through the cordon his foes had spread about him. During the night he had abandoned all his defences, and by daybreak he had taken the greater part of his army across the river Vid. Advancing along the Sophia road, he charged the Russian entrenchments with such energy that the Siberian Regiment stationed at that point was almost annihilated. A desperate fight went on for four hours, with the Russians coming up battalion after battalion. Some time after noon all firing ceased, and later the Turks sent up a white flag. Cheer after cheer swelled over the dreary plain. Osman had surrendered.

The siege had lasted one hundred and forty-two days. The Russians had lost forty thousand men. The Turks had lost thirty thousand men.

The advance on Constantinople had been checked. Skobeleff said, "Osman the Victorious he will remain, in spite of his surrender."

The Storming of
Burkersdorf Heights

FREDERICK THE GREAT AT BURKERSDORF

The Storming of Burkersdorf Heights

When, in 1740, Wilhelm Friedrich of Prussia died, the friends whom his heir had gathered about him at his pleasant country-house at Reinsberg were doomed to see a blight fall on their expectations such as had not been known since Poins and Falstaff congratulated themselves on having an old friend for their king.

When the young prince came to the throne as Frederick II., thought these trusting people, Prussia, instead of being a mere barracks, overrun with soldiers and ruled by a miser, would become the refuge of poets and artists. Its monarch would be a man of peace, caring for nothing beyond the joys of philosophy, poetry, music, and merry feasts—this, of course, providing for an indefinite extension of the enchanted life he and his companions led at Reinsberg.

They had the best of reasons for this belief: the antagonism between the prince and his father had begun almost as soon as the rapture of having an heir had become an old story to Friedrich Wilhelm. The tiny "Fritz," with a cocked hat and tight little soldier-clothes, drilling and being drilled with a lot of other tiny boys,—and frightfully bored with it all the time,—was a standing grievance to his rough, boorish father. "Awake him at six in the morning, and stand by to see that he does not turn over, but immediately gets up.... While his hair is being combed and made into a queue, he is to have his breakfast of tea." This was the beginning of his

43

father's instructions to his tutors when, at seven, he passed out of his governess's hands.

Notwithstanding the fine Spartan rigour of this programme, the boy came up a dainty, delicate little fellow, who turned up his nose at boar-hunting and despised his father's collection of giants, and loved to play the flute and make French verses. Friedrich Wilhelm was anything but a bad monarch; he was moral in a century when nothing of the sort was expected of monarchs; he made the Prussian army the best army in the world; he even had affections; but for a man of these virtues he was the most intolerable parent of whom there is a record.

The brilliant Wilhelmina, Frederick's dearly loved sister, whose young portraits show her as very like her brother, has this characteristic scene in her *Memoirs*. Their sister, Princess Louisa, aged fifteen, had just been betrothed to a margrave, and the king asked her—they were at table—how she would regulate her housekeeping when she was married. Louisa, a favourite, had got into the way of telling her father home-truths, which he took very well, as a rule, from her. On this occasion she told him that she would have a good table well served; "better than yours," said Louisa; "and if I have children, I will not maltreat them like you, nor force them to eat what they have an aversion to."

"What do you mean by that?" said the king. "What is there wanting at my table?"

"There is this wanting," she replied: "that one cannot have enough, and the little there is consists of coarse potherbs that nobody can eat."

The king, who was not used to such candour, boiled with rage. "All his anger," says the Princess Wilhelmina, "fell on my brother and me. He first threw a plate at my brother's head, who ducked out of the way, then let fly another at me." After he had made the air blue with wrath, directed at Frederick, "we had to pass him in going out," and "he aimed a great blow at me with his crutch,—which, if I had not jerked away from it, would have ended me. He chased me for a while in his wheelchair, but the people drawing it gave me time to escape into the queen's chamber." One always imagines this charming young princess in the act of dodging some sort of blow from Friedrich Wilhelm, who was nicknamed "Stumpy," privately, by his dutiful son and daughter. The habit of hating his son became an insanity; to kick him and pull his hair, break his flute, and take away his books and his brocaded dressing-gown—that was ordinary usage; it came to the point where he nearly strangled him, and later he condemned him to death for trying to run away to his uncle, George II., in England. When this sentence had been changed to a term of imprisonment, the poor young prince had a much better time of it: his gaolers were kinder than his father.

By the time he emerged from this captivity he had gained much wisdom—the cold wisdom of selfishness and dissimulation. In after years the father and son became profoundly attached to each other, but Frederick was always obliged to humour and cajole his pig-headed sire, to lie more or less, and generally adopt an insincere tone, in order to avert wrath and suspicion—a very hateful necessity to a natural truth-teller, for Frederick was by nature a great lover of facts. Although his training as a politician and a soldier included a thorough education in guile, the tutors of his childhood were simple, honest people, who gave him a good, truthful start in life.

Friedrich Wilhelm, now that his heir was twenty-one years old, thought it high time to put an end to various vague matrimonial projects, and get a wife for him straight away. Frederick having found that obedience was, on the whole, better than captivity, was submissive and silent—to his father; but his letters to his friends and his sister shrieked with protestations against a marriage in which his tastes and feelings were not so much as thought of. Above all things he wished to be allowed to travel and choose for himself, and he had a morbid horror of a dull and awkward woman. It did not much matter, he thought, what else his wife was if she were clever conversationally, with grace and charm and fine manners. Beauty was desirable, but he could get along without it, if only he could feel proud of his consort's wit and breeding. The bride of his father's choosing was the Princess Elizabeth of Brunswick-Bevern—a bashful and gawky young person, with as little distinction as a dairy-maid. But he subdued his rage and married her, and, indeed, seems always to have treated her with kindly deference, although he made no pretence of affection. Still carrying out his father's wishes, he served in a brief campaign, and afterwards regularly devoted a portion of his time to military and political business. Friedrich Wilhelm was now pleased with his son to the extent of buying for him a delightful residence—Reinsberg—and giving him a tolerable income; and Frederick revelled in his new freedom by building conservatories, laying out pleasure-gardens, playing his flute to his heart's content, writing poor French verses, and solacing himself for the "coarse potherbs" of his childhood by exquisite dinners. They had the best musicians for their concerts at Reinsberg—the crown prince and his friends, with the crown princess and her ladies. It was here, in 1736, that Frederick began—by letter—his famous friendship with Voltaire, that survived so many phases of illusion and disillusion.

It must be said of Frederick's friends—who were mostly French—that they were men of highly trained intelligence, but they were not acute enough to know what sort of king their prince would make.

When his father passed away, Frederick felt as sincere a grief as if there had never been anything but love between them; always afterwards he spoke of him with reverence and he learned to place a high value on the stern discipline of his early life—which is still to some extent a model for the bringing up of young Hohenzollerns.

It was a handsome young king who came to the throne

in 1740. His face was round, his nose a keen aquiline, his mouth small and delicately curved, and all was dominated by those wonderful blue-grey eyes, that, as Mirabeau said, "at the bidding of his heroic soul fascinated you with seduction or with terror." Even in youth the lines of the face showed a sardonic humour. One can well imagine his replying to the optimistic Sulzer, who thought severe punishments a mistake: "*Ach! meine lieber* Sulzer, you don't know this—race!" In the old-age portraits the face is sharp and hatchet-like, the mouth is shrunken to a mean line, but the great eyes still flash out, commanding and clear.

The reign began with peace and philanthropy: Frederick II. started out by disbanding the giant grenadiers, the absurd monstrosities that his father had begged and bought and kidnapped from everywhere; he started a "knitting-house" for a thousand old women; abolished torture in criminal trials; set up an Academy of Sciences; summoned Voltaire and Maupertius; made Germany open its eyes at the speech, "In this country every man must get to Heaven in his own way"; and proclaimed a practical freedom of the press—all in his first week.

The fury of activity now took possession of Frederick, which lasted all his life. He had the Hohenzollern passion for doing everything himself: the three "secretaries of state" were mere clerks, who spared him only the mechanical part of secretarial duties. His system of economy was rigid. While looking over financial matters one day he found that a certain convent absorbed a considerable fund from the forest-dues, which had been bequeathed by dead dukes "for masses to be said on their behalf." He went to the place and asked the monks, "What good does anybody get out of those masses?"

"Your majesty, the dukes are to be delivered out of purgatory by them."

"Purgatory? And they are not out yet, poor souls, after so many hundred years of praying?"

The answer was, "Not yet."

"When will they be out, and the thing settled?" There was no answer to this. "Send me a courier whenever they are out!" With this sneer the king left the convent.

Stern business went on all day, and in the evening, music, dancing, theatres, suppers, till all hours; but the king was up again at four in the summer—five in winter. In early youth Frederick had known a period of gross living, from which he suffered so severely that his reaction from it was fiercely austere. After his accession, a young man who had been associated with this "mud-bath," as Carlyle has named it, begged an audience. The king received him, but rebuked him with such withering speech that he straightway went home and killed himself.

Only five months of his reign had passed when the event occurred that put an end to the ideal monarch of Frederick's subjects. Charles VI., Emperor of Germany, was dead. For years he had worked to bind together his scattered and wobbling empire, and by his "Pragmatic Sanction" secure it to his daughter, Maria Theresa, contrary to the rule that only male heirs should succeed, and she was on the day of his death (October 20) proclaimed empress.

If the young Maria Theresa had been married to the young Prince Frederick of Prussia, as their reigning parents had at one time decided, European history would undoubtedly have been different, though historians may be mistaken in thinking that much trouble would have been saved the world. In view of the fact that both these young people were extravagantly well endowed with the royal gifts of energy and decision, one must be permitted to wonder whether Frederick, as the spouse of the admirable Maria Theresa, would have ever become known as "the Great." But at all events it would have prevented him from rushing in on her domains and seizing Silesia as soon as she was left with no one but her husband—a man of the kindly inert sort—to protect her; and we should have lost the good historical scene of Maria Theresa appearing before her Hungarian Diet, with the crown on her beautiful head, thrilling every heart as she lifted her plump baby, Francis Joseph, and with tears streaming down her face implored its help against the Prussian robber.

We can still hear the thunderous roar of the loyal reply, "We will die for our sovereign, Maria Theresa!"

Nevertheless, by December the Prussian robber was in Silesia with thirty thousand men, engaged in finding out that he was really made to be a warrior. By May he held every fortified place in the province; by June Maria Theresa was forced to cede it to him—since which time it has always been a loyal part of Prussia. "How glorious is my king, the youngest of the kings and the grandest!" chanted Voltaire in a letter to Frederick, who, one is pleased to know, found the praise rather suffocating.

The genius of Frederick was next put to a considerable test in the way of matchmaking—a delicate art, particularly when practised for the sake of providing the half-barbarous empire of Russia with mated rulers.

The Czarina Elizabeth—Great Peter's daughter—wished the king to find a German bride for her nephew-heir, who was afterwards Peter III. A true Hohenzollern, Frederick felt himself quite equal to this task—as to any other. From a bevy of young princesses he selected the daughter of the poverty-stricken Prince of Anhalt-Herbst, because of the unmistakable cleverness the girl had shown, though not fifteen. She was handsome as well, and Elizabeth renamed her "Catherine," changed her religion, and the marriage came off in 1745. Frederick had displayed great acumen, but it would puzzle a fiend to contrive a more diabolical union than that of Peter and Catherine!

Meanwhile, Maria Theresa had been preparing to fight for Silesia again. Without waiting for her, Frederick pounced upon Prague and captured it. After her armies in Silesia and Saxony had been put to flight by her adversary, at Hohenfriedberg and Sorr, and Hennersdorf and Kesselsdorf, the empress yielded. On Christmas Day, 1745, when the treaty was signed that gave Silesia again to Prussia,—it was known as the Peace of Dresden,—Berlin

went wild, and for the first time shouts were heard among the revellers, "*Vivat Friedrich der Grosse!*" The Austrians might call him "that ferocious, false, ambitious king of Prussia," but as a matter of fact he was not more false and ferocious than the other rulers, only infinitely more able. Frederick had made for himself a great name and raised his little kingdom—of only two and a half millions of people—to a noble standing among nations. The eyes of the world were fixed upon the hero to see what he would do next. What he did was to swear that he "would not fight with a cat again," and to build himself a charming country home—his palaces, and even Reinsberg, were too large. In May, 1747, he had his housewarming at little Sans Souci, where for the next forty years most of his time was spent. There were twenty boxes of German flutes in the king's cabinet at Sans Souci, and infinite boxes of Spanish snuff; and there were three arm-chairs for three favourite dogs, with low stools to make an easy step for them. There was another favourite at Sans Souci who was said to look like an ape, although he was mostly called the "skinny Apollo." How one would like to have seen the king walking the terraces, with "white shoes and stockings and red breeches, with gown and waistcoat of blue linen flowered and lined with yellow!" while men with powdered wigs and highly coloured clothes, and women whose heads bore high towers of hair unpleasantly stuffed and decorated with inconsequent dabs of finery, followed him, all talking epigrams and doing attitudes—polite people had to hold themselves in curves in the eighteenth century.

These were good years for Prussia: her law courts were reformed; her commerce flourished, and so did agriculture; potatoes were introduced—they were at first considered poisonous; a huge amount of building was done, and the army was drilled constantly under Frederick's eyes. Each year saw it a better army; its chief must have known that he was preparing for the great struggle of his life, although he took as keen an interest in keeping up the high standard of his new opera-house in Berlin, both as to music and ballet, as he did in the skilfullest manoeuvres of his troops.

Maria Theresa had never for a moment given up Silesia in her heart. She was a woman of austere virtues, but these did not stand in the way of schemes which she would have thought too despicable to be used against any one but the King of Prussia. The Czarina of Russia had been made to hate him by a series of carefully-devised plots,—she looked on him as her arch-enemy,—and within six months after the Peace of Dresden she had signed, with Maria Theresa, a treaty which actually proposed the partitioning of Frederick's, kingdom, which was to be divided between Russia, Austria, and Poland, while he was to become a simple Margrave of Brandenburg!

To get the signature of Louis XV. involved harder work still for the virtuous empress—but she did it. It was to ask it of the Pompadour—in various affectionate letters, beginning "My dear cousin," or "Madame, my dearest sister." The Pompadour was also shown some stinging verses of Frederick's with herself as subject, and she (representing France) became the firm ally of Maria Theresa.

Through an Austrian clerk's treachery Frederick became aware of this stupendous conspiracy against him—but not till 1755, when it was well matured. It seemed incredible that he could think of keeping these great countries from gobbling up his little state. He could not have done it, indeed, if it had not been for a certain Englishman. It was an Englishman who saved Frederick and Prussia—the "Great Commoner," Pitt, who, having on hand a French war of his own, raised a Hanoverian army to help himself and Frederick, and granted him a welcome subsidy of six hundred and seventy thousand pounds a year.

His ten years' drilling had given Frederick a fine army of one hundred and thirty thousand men. The infantry were said to excel all others in quickness of manoeuvres and skilled shooting, while the cavalry was unsurpassed.

Frederick, without waiting for his foes to declare war and mass their mighty forces, began it by a stealthy, sudden move into Saxony in September 1756. October 1, at Lowositz, in Bohemia, he defeated von Browne, and, returning, captured the Saxon force of seventeen thousand, and took them bodily—all but the officers—into his own army.

England was delighted with this masterly act of her ally. He was known there as "the Protestant hero," which was not quite true to facts. Certainly Frederick protested against the old religion, but he was far from being on with the new one. His saying, "Every one shall go to heaven in the way he chooses," had been applauded in England, but they were not familiar with his reply when a squabble as to whether one or another set of hymn-books should be used was referred to him: "Bah! let them sing what tomfoolery they like," said the "Protestant hero." Had France and Austria, however, succeeded in obliterating Prussia, it is likely that Protestantism too would have been done for in Germany.

Frederick having himself begun the Seven Years' War, the confederated German states, with Russia, France, and Sweden, formally bound themselves to "reduce the House of Brandenburg to its former state of mediocrity," France—very rich then—paying enormous subsidies all around. England—with Hanover—alone espoused Prussia's cause. During 1757, four hundred and thirty-seven thousand men were put in the field against Frederick. Only his cat-like swiftness saved him from being overwhelmed again and again. In April he made another rush—like an avalanche—on Bohemia, and won another great victory at Prague, but he was terribly beaten by General Daun in June at Kolin. Still he kept up courage, and played the flute and wrote innumerable French verses of the usual poor quality in odd moments. In November, at Rossbach, he met an army of French and Imperialists over twice as large as his own, and by a swift, unexpected movement broke them, so that they were scattered all over the country. Every German felt proud of this French defeat, whether he were Prussian or not. It was the first time the invincible French had ever been beaten by a wholly German army, with a leader of German blood. The brilliant victory of Leuthen followed Rossbach.

But although the world was ringing with Frederick's name, and he was acknowledged to be one of the greatest generals of history, the resources of his powerful enemies were too many for him. At last it seemed that a ruinous cloud of disaster was closing around him and darkening the memory of his glorious successes.

The defeat of Kunersdorf in 1759 would have completely wiped out his army if the over-cautious Austrian General Daun had followed up his victory. "Is there no cursed bullet that can reach me!" the Prussian monarch was heard to murmur in a stupor of despair after the battle. He carried poison about him, after this, to use when affairs became too bad. A severe blow followed Kunersdorf,—George II. died in October 1760; George III. put an end to Pitt's ministry—and this was the end of England's support.

The winter of 1761-1762 saw Frederick at his lowest ebb. England's money had stopped; his own country, plundered, devastated in every direction, afforded no sufficient revenue. Fully half of the Prussian dominions were occupied by the enemy; men, horses, supplies, and transport could hardly be procured. The Prussian army was reduced to sixty thousand men, and its ranks were made up largely of vagabonds and deserters—the old, splendidly disciplined troops having been practically obliterated.

He played no more on his flute—poor Frederick! At Leipzig an old friend sighed to him, "Ach! how lean your majesty has grown!"

"Lean, *ja wohl*," he replied; "and what wonder, with three women (Pompadour, Maria Theresa, and Czarina Elizabeth) hanging to my throat all this while!"

The Allies felt that it was only a matter of a short time before they should see their great enemy humbled to the position of Elector of Brandenburg. From this abasement Frederick was suddenly saved in January 1762. Life held another chance for him. The implacable old czarina was dead; her heir, Peter III., was not merely the friend, but the enthusiastic adorer of Frederick of Prussia. Although thirty-four years old and the husband of Catherine (the young lady Frederick had taken such pains to select for him so many years ago), Peter had been kept out of public affairs as if he were a child. Neither he nor Catherine was allowed to leave the palace without permission of the czarina; they were surrounded with spies, and kept in a gaudy and dirty semi-imprisonment—the traditional style for heirs to the Russian throne. Under this system they became masters of deceit. Catherine, in her cleverly unpleasant *Memoirs,* tells how they managed to escape and visit people without being found out; how she, when ill and in bed, had a joyous company with her, who huddled behind a screen when prying ladies-in-waiting entered. But the most painful part is the account of Peter, who seems to have had more versatility in hateful ways than any one outside of Bedlam. Crazily vivacious over foolish games, brutal when drunk, and silly when sober, one wonders how for so many years Catherine endured him.

There was a saving grace, though, in him: he worshipped the King of Prussia.

Frederick adroitly rose to the occasion: releasing all his Russian prisoners, he sent them, well clad and provisioned, back to their country. On February 23 the czar responded by a public declaration of peace with Prussia and a renunciation of all conquests made during the war. His general, Czernichef, was ordered to put himself and his twenty thousand men at the disposal of the Prussian hero, and on May 5 a treaty of alliance between Prussia and Russia was announced—to the horror and disgust of France and Austria. They had relied on Czernichef, but Czernichef himself was a sincere admirer of his new commander-in-chief and delighted in the change. The Russian soldiers all shared this feeling: they called Frederick "Son of the lightning."

The French were being held by the Hanoverian army; Sweden had retired from the war; with Russia on his side, Frederick felt that he might hold out against Austria till peace was declared by the powers—peace with no provision made for the partition of his kingdom.

In planning his next campaign—the last of the war—it was evident to Frederick that nothing could be done without recapturing the fortress of Schweidnitz, recently captured by Loudon, the Austrian general. The Austrians held all Silesia, and they must be put out of it, but with Schweidnitz in their hands this was impossible.

Fortunately for Frederick, Daun was appointed commander-in-chief of the Austrians, the general who had been execrated throughout the empire for his failure to follow up Frederick after Kunersdorf. In mid-May Daun took command of the forces in Silesia, and with an army of seventy thousand men made haste to place himself in a strong position among rugged hills to guard Schweidnitz. Schweidnitz, with a garrison of twelve thousand picked men and firm defences, it was impossible to attack while Daun was there. Frederick made repeated efforts to force Daun to give up his hold on the fortress, threatening his left wing, as his right wing seemed impregnably situated; but Daun, although forced to change his position from time to time, kept firmly massed about Schweidnitz. Frederick at last, then, resolved to attempt the impossible, and, his forces now augmented by Czernichef's to eighty-one thousand, determined on storming the Heights of Burkersdorf, where Daun's right wing was firmly entrenched.

The last of Frederick's notable battles of the war,—a conflict upon which the destinies of Prussia turned,—it was planned and executed by him with a consummate brightness and cleverness that more than justifies the Hohenzollern worship of their great ancestor.

Burkersdorf Height, near the village of the same name, which was also occupied by Daun, lies parallel to Kunersdorf Heights, where Frederick's army lay. It is a high hill, very steep, and half covered with rugged underbrush on the side next to Frederick's position, and Prince de Ligne and General O'Kelly—serving under Daun—had made it bristle with guns. Artillery was Daun's specialty; his guns were thick wherever the ground was not impractically steep, and palisades— "the pales strong as masts and room only for a musket-barrel between"—protected the soldiery; they were even "furnished with a lath or cross-strap all along for resting the gun-barrel on and taking aim." In fact, Burkersdorf Height was as good as a fortress. East of it was a small valley where strong entrenchments had been made and batteries placed. Farther east, two other heights had to be captured,—they were also well defended,—Ludwigsdorf and Leuthmannsdorf.

By the 17th of July Frederick had all his plans matured, and had made his very first move—that is, he had sent Generals Mollendorf and Wied on a march with their men to put the enemy on a false scent—when he received a call from Czernichef at his headquarters. It was paralysing news that Czernichef brought: Peter, the providential friend, had been dethroned by the partisans of his clever wife, Catherine.

After a reign of six months the young czar had completely disgusted his subjects: he had planned ambitious schemes of reform, and at the same time had made despotic encroachments. After delighting the Church with important concessions, he proposed virtually to take away all its lands and houses. He overdid everything, like the madman he was. He offended his army by dressing up his guards in Prussian uniforms and teaching them the Prussian drill, while he wore constantly the dress of a Prussian colonel, and sang the praises of our hero until his people were sick of the name of "my friend, the King of Prussia." Russian morals in the eighteenth century were like snakes in Ireland—there were none. In this respect Catherine was not superior to her husband, but in mental gifts she was an extraordinary young woman. Her tact, her poise, her intelligence, would have made a noble character in a decent atmosphere. Peter had recognised her powers and relied on them, and she had endured him all these years, thinking she would one day rule Russia as his empress. But since his accession he had been completely under the dominion of the Countess Woronzow, a vicious creature, who meant to be Catherine's successor. And Catherine, when Peter threatened her and her son Paul with lifelong imprisonment, had on her side finally begun a plot, which resulted in her appealing to the guards, much as Maria Theresa had appealed to her Diet of Hungary. Every one was tired of Peter, and no voice was raised against his deposition, whereupon Catherine assumed the sovereignty of Russia, to the great relief and satisfaction of all Russians. The brutal assassination of poor Peter by Catherine's friends—not by her orders—followed in a few days.

It was the intention of Catherine, on beginning her reign, to restore Elizabeth's policy in Russian matters and recommence hostilities against Frederick; but on looking over Peter's papers she found that Frederick had discouraged his wild schemes, and that he had begged him to rely on his wife and respect her counsels, and this produced a revulsion of feeling. She resolved that she would not fight him; nor, on the other hand, would she be his ally; the secret message that had come to Czernichef, and which he communicated to Frederick, was that Catherine reigned, and that he, her general, was ordered to return immediately to St. Petersburg.

One can only guess at Frederick's emotions at this news. Life must have seemed a lurid melodrama, presenting one hideous act after another. "This is not living," he said; "this is being killed a thousand times a day!" On the eve of the attack on Burkersdorf his ally had been taken away from him; his own forces were now weaker than those of Daun, and he did not see his way to a victory.

But the genius of Frederick could not allow him to give in to the destinies. His resourcefulness came to his rescue. He simply begged Czernichef to stay with him for three days. Three days must elapse before his official commands came. Frederick, with all the potency of his personal fascination, implored the Russian during that time to keep the matter secret, and, without one hostile act against the enemy, to *seem* to act with him as though their relations were unchanged. Czernichef consented; it was one of the most devoted acts that was ever done by a man for pure friendship; he well knew, and so did Frederick, that he might lose his head or rot in a dungeon for it, but—his own heroism was great enough to make the sacrifice.

The drama accordingly went on. On the evening of the 20th, with the forces of Mollendorf and Wied, who had puzzled the enemy and returned, with Ziethen and Czernichef,—this last, of course, only for show,—Frederick silently marched into Burkersdorf village and took by storm the old Burkersdorf Castle,—an affair of a few hours,—while Daun's forces fled in all directions from the village. Then, through the night, trenches were dug and batteries built—forty guns well placed. At sunrise the whole Prussian army could be seen to be in motion by their opponents.

At four o'clock Frederick's famous cannonade began, concentrated upon the principal height of Burkersdorf. General O'Kelly's men were too high to be reached by the cannon, but it was Frederick's object to keep a furious, confusing noise going on, to help to draw attention from Wied and Mollendorf, who were doing the real fighting of the day. Mollendorf was to storm O'Kelly's height, and Wied the Ludwigsdorf height beyond; but Frederick had arranged a spectacular drama by which the foe was to be deceived as to these intentions. It was not for nothing that Frederick had personally overlooked his theatres and operas all these years. His knowledge of scenic displays and their effect on the minds of an audience stood him in good stead this day.

The Prussian guns continued a deafening roar, hour after hour, with many blank charges, and the bewildered commanders of the allied Austrians watched from their elevation the small man on his white horse giving orders right and left. He wore a three-cornered hat with a white feather, a plain blue uniform with red facings, a yellow waistcoat liberally powdered with Spanish snuff, black velvet breeches, and high soft boots. They were shabby old clothes, but the figure had a majesty that every one recognised. The difficulty among the officers on the heights was to find out what were the orders Frederick was giving so freely. His generals, who were much smarter in their dress than he, dashed off in all directions, and marched their troops briskly about, keeping the whole line of the enemy on the alert.

Daun, ignorant of the St. Petersburg revolution and its consequences, and seeing the Russian masses drawn up threateningly opposite his left wing, which he commanded, dared not concentrate his whole force on Burkersdorf, but from time to time sent bodies of men to support de Ligne and O'Kelly. As no one could tell what spot to support, no line of action could be agreed upon. The commandant of Schweidnitz, General Guasco, with twelve thousand men, came out of the fortress to attack the Prussian rear, but, fortunately for Frederick, one of his astute superiors sent him back.

Meantime, while this uproar and these puzzling operations were going on, Wied had taken his men out of view of the Austrians by circuitous paths to the gradual eastern ascent of Ludwigsdorf and moved up in three detachments. Battery after battery he dislodged, but when he came in sight of the huge mass of guns and men at the top, it seemed wild foolishness to try to get there. It could never have been done by a straight, headlong rush; they crawled along through thickets and little valleys, creeping spirally higher and higher, dodging the fire from above, till at last a movement through a dense wood brought them to the rear and flank of the foe. Then, with a magnificent charge of bayonets, they sent them flying, and passed on to the easy rout of the troops on Leuthmannsdorf.

On Burkersdorf Height O'Kelly's men were looking for an attack on the steepest side, where they were best fortified, but Möllendorf's troops had gone by a roundabout route to the western slope, where after some searching they found a sheep-track winding up the hillside. Following this, they came to a slope so steep that horses could not draw the guns. And then the men pushed and pulled them along and up, until the Austrians spied them from above, and the cannon-balls came crashing down into them. But under this fire they planted their guns, and did such gallant work with them that they were soon at the top, dashing down the defences. It was a tough struggle: the defences were strong—there were line after line of them—and the Austrians had no idea of yielding. They fought like tigers until the fire from the muskets set the dry branches of their abatis ablaze, and Mollendorf quickly closed in around them and forced them to surrender. Frederick's orchestra still boomed on, and the show of officers on prancing steeds and parading troops kept reinforcements from coming to assist the men on Burkersdorf.

It was noon when Mollendorf had achieved his task, and Daun ordered the army to fall back. But Frederick kept his cannon going as if with a desperate intention till five, to make matters appear more dangerous than they really were to Daun. He was successful; at nightfall Daun led his entire army away, silently and in order, and he never troubled Frederick again.

He left fourteen guns behind him and over one thousand prisoners, and quite two thousand deserted to Frederick in the next few days.

And Czernichef, who had stood by him so nobly? He was full of warmest admiration for Frederick's curious tactics and their success, and the king must have been eternally grateful to him. He marched for home early next morning—and he was neither beheaded nor imprisoned by Catherine when he got there: one is very glad to know that.

Frederick was now enabled to besiege Schweidnitz; its reconquest gave him back Silesia and left him to long years of peace at Sans Souci. It is fair to conclude that these were happy years, since his happiness lay in incessant work; it needed the most arduous toil to get his country into shape again, but Prussia deserved it—"To have achieved a Frederick the Second for king over it was Prussia's great merit," says Carlyle.

The Battle of Leipzig

LEIPZIG—GUSTAVUS ADOLPHUS GIVING THANKS FOR VICTORY

The Battle of Leipzig

At the opening of the seventeenth century the prospects of Sweden must have seemed to offer less hope than those of any nation of Europe.

Only a scanty population clung to the land, whose long winters paralysed its industrial activities for many months of the year; and the deadly proximity of the insolent conqueror, Denmark, cut her off almost entirely from European commerce and made her complete subjugation seem but a question of time.

Then it was that the powerful Gustavus Vasa took charge of Sweden's destinies, delivering the country from Danish tyranny and establishing his new monarchy with the Lutheran Church for its foundation.

He was the first of a great race of kings. From the beginning of his reign, 1527, to the death of Charles XII., 1718, every monarch displayed some signal ability. But the finest flower of the line, the most original genius and hero, and one of the world's greatest conquerors, was Gustavus Adolphus, the "Northern Lion."

He was the grandson of the liberator, Gustavus Vasa, the first Protestant prince ever crowned, and the son of Charles IX., who came to the throne in his son's tenth year.

Gustavus Adolphus was born in 1594, his advent bringing great joy to the Swedes, as it shut out the possible accession of the Polish house of Vasa, who were Roman Catholics. From early childhood it was apparent that he had unusual qualities of mind, great steadfastness, and high ideals of duty, while his perceptions were swift and wonderfully luminous.

From the first he was inured to hardships—early rising, simple fare, indifference to heat and cold; much the same sort of discipline, I suppose, to which the boys of the house of Hohenzollern are now habituated. His father felt the necessity of securing the most distinguished men that were to be found for his son's education, both from Sweden and foreign lands. Count de la Gardie had charge of his military education; Helmer von Morner, of Brandenburg, was his teacher in science and languages, and John Skythe, a man of great learning, had general charge. So much severe military drill, combined with constant lessons perseveringly administered by intellectual martinets, has had the effect of crushing the spontaneity, the power of taking the initiative, out of many a callow princeling; but Gustavus was not of any ordinary princely metal. He took kindly to handling a musket and playing soldier, while at the same time he displayed a wonderful facility for learning anything that was presented to him.

Besides his mother tongue, he understood Greek, Latin, German, Dutch, Italian, Polish, and Russian, using Latin in daily speech with special fluency. His vigorous memory and brilliantly keen understanding were at the service of his natural desire to know, and all combined to make the work of teaching him a delight.

His father was proud of the promise he showed, and from his tenth year onward allowed him to take part in his councils and audiences, and sometimes even to give his answers in council. Records of reports of foreign ambassadors contain many praises of his intelligence and keen discernment in abstruse questions. When he visited Heidelberg in 1620 the Duke of Zweibriicken gave an extremely admiring account of him.

Mathematics came to him easily. His favourite subjects were the various branches of military science, and fortifications, their plans and erection, exercised his mind almost unceasingly. Grotius's treatise on the *Right of War and Peace* and Xenophon's *Anabasis* were among his favourite readings.

The family of Adolphus owed their position as the reigning power of the country to their espousal of Protestant principles, and it was therefore considered essential that the youth should be brought up to consider himself as the champion and defender of the Protestant faith.

But it seemed a part of his very being to feel sympathy with this belief only. He indeed seemed to have been born an ardent Protestant. The fine austerity of his temperament, the elevation and purity of his mind, made it impossible for him ever to relax his views. Protestantism, or Lutheranism, as the latest form of religion of which he was aware, excited his sincere devotion, which throughout his career only grew to greater heights of self-effacing enthusiasm.

Gustavus is described as being tall and slim in his early youth, with a long, thin, pale face, light hair, and pointed beard. But in after years he grew to great height and bulk, and is said to have been extremely slow and clumsy in his movements, and so heavy that no Swedish horse could carry him in armour.

It is a curious physical fact in connection with this indisputable one that his mind formed its lucid conclusions like lightning, and that much of his success as a soldier was due to the marvellous speed of his operations.

His portrait, taken at this later period by Van Dyke, shows the long face well rounded; the nose is of the prominent Roman type, while the pointed beard is still worn, also a moustache curved up at the ends. The eyes are large and beautifully shaped; they were steel-grey, and capable of fearful flashes of anger when the quick and often-repented temper of the monarch was aroused; but the brows are finely arched, and the whole face expresses justice and benevolence. Sternness is in it, but it is the face pre-eminently of a good man. One can read in it the courage of high principles and a great mind; it is absolutely unlike the portraits of the ferocious and dissolute warriors of the time.

His first campaign was undertaken when he was only in his seventeenth year. He stormed the city of Christianople, which then belonged to Denmark, and triumphantly entered the town, but afterwards, when attacking one of the Danish islands, the young leader came to grief; his horse broke through the thin ice over a morass, where he floundered for some time, surrounded by his enemies. He was finally rescued by young Baner.

In the same year Charles IX. died, and the queen-dowager, the stepmother of Gustavus, having made a full resignation of her claims to the regency, which under Swedish law she might have claimed until Gustavus had reached his twenty-fourth year, he succeeded to his father's title of "King Elect of the Swedes, Goths, and Vandals."

For a young man of eighteen it was a formidable undertaking to ascend the throne of Sweden, and he behaved with modesty and dignity at a session of the States Assembly convened to discuss the rights of succession. He spoke of his youth and inexperience, but added manfully, "Nevertheless, if the States persist. in making me king, I will endeavour to acquit myself with honour and fidelity."

He was formally proclaimed king on December 31, 1611.

All the force of his character was now called into play. Among the nobility there was a great deal of jealousy; people of a certain rank felt that there was no reason why he should occupy the throne—each of them had quite as good a claim to it as this grandson of a former subject.

But here Gustavus's great personal force made itself apparent. The malcontents found it impossible to treat him otherwise than with the respect due to a sovereign. He was able to control his natural impetuosity in all matters of court usage; his nobles were first made to feel that they were kept at a distance and under the dominion of a powerful will, and then they seemed glad to serve him as he wished. His appointments of men to fill public posts, civil and military, showed remarkable acumen. For his principal counsellor he chose the famous Oxenstiern, distinguished at twenty-eight as the coldest, most practical of diplomats, and who has left a reputation as an unequalled statesman.

Two sets of questions now presented themselves to the king and the Senate: one related to the development of agriculture and mining in the country, the other to the critical condition of the kingdom, between Danes, Polanders, and Muscovites.

The king decided to continue the war with Denmark, but as King Christian got the better of him, he astutely receded, and signed a treaty of peace in 1613. He then proceeded against the Czar of Muscovy, and thereby augmented the Swedish kingdom by several provinces of importance, one of which included the ground on which St. Petersburg now stands.

In 1617 peace was concluded with Russia through the mediation of James I. of England, who was always offering himself as a peacemaker.

Gustavus now went through the ceremonies of a coronation at Upsal. It is said that this brief time of festivity was the only rest he ever enjoyed from the end of his childhood to the abrupt close of his life. At this time of so-called rest, indeed, he was concentrating all his mind on international affairs, studying the laws of commerce, and trying to lift the burden of taxation from his people as far as was possible.

He looked over his ships, which were in a wretched condition as a whole, and sent for the best mariners he could obtain from Holland and the Hanse Towns, with the idea of building up a good and sufficient navy.

His army also profited by his inventions in arms and artillery; indeed, he had at all times a watchful eye upon his soldiers, providing for their comfort and well-being. They had fur-lined coats for cold weather, and comfortable tents, and they could take the field in the bitterest winter as well as in summer.

Sweden was continually exporting steel for armour to Spain and Italy, so it occurred to Gustavus to establish home manufactories of firearms and swords that should equal those of any other country. Among his many useful improvements and inventions the leather cannon was the most curious. These pieces, being very light, were easily shifted on the battle-field and rapidly hauled over rugged country. They were made of thick layers of the hardest leather girt around with iron or brass hoops. After a dozen discharges they would fall to pieces, but they were made in camp in quantities, and could be replaced at once. Gustavus attributed many of his most brilliant victories to them and used them till the day of his death.

At this time the king and Oxenstiern were staying for a time at a castle which he had inherited from a cousin, when a fire broke out in the night and raged up all the staircases. They could only save themselves by jumping out of the windows and wading up to their shoulders through a filthy moat, but both escaped with nothing worse than bruises.

Schiller speaks admiringly of Gustavus for "a glorious triumph over himself by which he began a reign which was but one continued series of triumphs, and which was terminated by a victory."

This triumph of duty over inclination was Gustavus's yielding to the entreaties of his stepmother and other counsellors and giving up the beautiful Emma, Countess of Brahe. He was deeply in love with her,—the chroniclers assure us that his intentions were honourable,—and she had promised to be his wife; but it was represented to him that although the Countess of Brahe had all the necessary merits and virtues, marriage with a subject would seriously impair the power of his throne. So, to quote Schiller again, he "regained an absolute ascendancy over a heart which the tranquillity of a domestic life was far from being able to satisfy."

His marriage, however, although it was dictated by considerations of policy, seems to have been a successful one.

In the summer of 1620 Gustavus made a tour, incognito, of the principal towns of Germany, with the object of seeing for himself, in Berlin, the sister of the elector. His suit prospered, and it is said that in defiance of the elector's wishes the Princess Maria Eleonora, who was then in her twentieth year, accepted Gustavus and eloped with him to Sweden. They were married in Stockholm with great pomp. She was graceful and majestic, and we are assured that she made Gustavus a worthy and Christian queen.

The relations of Sweden with Poland were perpetually unsatisfactory. Sigismund, its Catholic king, disputed the throne with his cousin Gustavus, and a tedious eight years' war resulted.

But instead of exhausting Sweden, it had the effect of developing the consummate military genius of her king; of bringing his army, by its constant exercise, to an extraordinary degree of skill, and of making ready for the coming great struggle in Germany the new principles of military art introduced by Gustavus.

Not only was he a brilliant strategist, but the king looked after his army with paternal care; it was well fed, well clad, and promptly and well paid. Every detail was attended to by him. Religious services were held, morning and evening, by every regiment. No plunder, cruelty, intemperance, no low and slanderous talk or immorality, were allowed—his officers And soldiers alike were obliged to follow his example.

It is not to be wondered at that this army was led from one victory to another, Or that the fame of its discipline and its Successes should be noised all over Europe. The great Thirty Years' War, that stupendous struggle of Roman Catholicism to blot out the work of the Reformation in Germany, was now raging, and in the various Protestant countries, notably England and Holland, as well as the anti-Papist states of Ger-

71

many, people were beginning to look towards Gustavus as the most likely champion to give them victory. There were no such generals on the Protestant side in Europe, and it was known that Gustavus was deeply and sincerely religious, leading an upright life—a man of honour, who might be relied upon to keep his word.

Ferdinand, the Catholic Emperor of Germany, laughed at the idea of the Swedish champion; the "Snow King," he said (this being one of the favourite names for Gustavus), would melt if he tried coming south.

As for Gustavus, he had longed for years to try conclusions with Tilly and the other Imperial generals, but more particularly since Ferdinand in 1629 had promulgated the Edict of Restitution, whereby at one stroke the Archbishoprics of Magdeburg and Bremen, the Bishoprics of Min-den, Verden, Halberstadt, Lubeck, Ratzeburg, Misnia, Merseburg, Naumburg, Brandenburg, Havelberg, Lebus, and Cammin, with one hundred and twenty smaller foundations, were taken away from the Protestant Church and restored to the Roman Catholic Church.

To restore these lands and dignities, which had been from fifty to eighty years in the possession of the Protestants, was of course impossible without the use of brute force. By using the armies of Tilly and Wallenstein to compel it, the Emperor Ferdinand proclaimed himself the author of a political and religious revolution, the success of which must depend entirely upon military despotism, and which was Without any moral basis whatever.

There were many different motives prompting Gustavus to enter the lists against Ferdinand's forces. It was not only that there was great flattery in the appeal to help the oppressed— not only that war was his native element, wherein he felt sure of success; besides all this, he had bitter grievances to redress. In 1629 Ferdinand sent sixteen thousand Imperialist troops to take part against him in the war with Poland. To Gustavus's remonstrance Wallenstein had replied, "The Emperor has too many soldiers; he must assist his good friends with them." The envoys sent to represent Gustavus at the Congress of Lubeck were insolently turned away. Ferdinand also continued to support the claims of the Polish king, Sigismund, to the Swedish throne, refused the title of king to Gustavus Adolphus, insulted the Swedish flag, and intercepted the king's despatches.

However, Gustavus would enter the war only at his own time and on his own terms. He was far too prudent and wise, far too dutiful, to impoverish his own country or leave her exposed to the attacks of enemies. In 1624 England had approached him, wishing to know his terms for invading Germany, but England would not accede to his rather high stipulations.

The King of Denmark then underbid Gustavus, made terms with England, and rushed into the German conflict with great confidence, but he was ignominiously defeated, while Wallenstein (at that time Ferdinand's best general) established himself on the Baltic coast. This was getting dangerously near, as Gustavus felt.

In 1628 Gustavus Adolphus made an alliance with Christian of Denmark, his old enemy, but as a Protestant and a foe to Catholic rule in Germany his loyal friend—for the time. It was agreed between them that all foreign ships except the ships of the Dutch should be excluded from the Baltic. In the summer of the same year he sent two thousand men to defend Stralsund against Wallenstein.

In 1629, through the secret intervention of Cardinal Richelieu, a treaty of peace was signed with Poland at Stuhmsdorf. Again, in 1630, Cardinal Richelieu, the wily diplomatist who governed France for Louis XIII. and had a hand in all the affairs of Europe, sent Baron de Charnace to Gustavus at Stockholm and made the same proposals in the name of France that England had made in 1624. But the flippant manner of de Charnace disgusted the king, and the terms did not please him: he did not care to assume the role of a mercenary general paid by France and bound for a limited number of years, and so de Charnace returned home without having accomplished anything.

Richelieu, as the minister of a Catholic king and a prince himself of the Roman Catholic Church, of course did not dare to openly ally himself with Gustavus in the latter's character of defender of the Protestant faith. But in his desire to frustrate the ambitions of the House of Austria, against which he had schemed for years, he was quite willing to support any power that would directly or indirectly advance the supremacy of France.

Gustavus now felt comparatively free to leave Sweden and invade Germany. By his treaty with Denmark he was free to retreat through her territory.

After the unsuccessful attempt made by Christian of Denmark to oppose the emperor by leading the forces of the Protestant Union, Gustavus remained the only prince in Europe to whom the Germans felt they could appeal—the only one strong enough to protect them, and upright enough to ensure them religious liberty.

Pressing appeals came from all sides now to add to his own personal motives for embarking in the German war. He raised an army of forty-three thousand men in Sweden, but set out on his expedition with only thirteen thousand. On the occasion of taking his leave, Gustavus appeared before the Estates with his little daughter of four in his arms. This princess was born so "dark and ugly," with such a "rough, loud voice," that the attendants had rushed to Gustavus with the news that a son was born to him. When this was found to be a mistake they were reluctant to tell him, as his joy at having an heir to his military greatness was so openly expressed. But finally his sister, the Princess Catherine, took the child to him and explained that it was a daughter. If he felt any disappointment he did not show it; tenderly kissing the child, he said, "Let us thank God, sister; I hope this girl will be as good as a boy; I am content, and pray God to preserve the child." Then, laughing, he added, "She is an arch wench, to put a trick upon us so soon."

In this manner did the celebrated Christina of Sweden enter the world. Her father was deeply fond of her, and enjoyed taking her to his reviews; there she showed great pleasure in hearing the salutes fired, clapping her little hands, so that the king would order the firing to be repeated for her, saying, "She is a soldier's daughter."

There is a famous letter of Gustavus's still preserved in which he wrote to Oxenstiern:

I exhort and entreat you, for the love of Christ, that if all does not go on well, you will not lose courage. I conjure you to remember me and the welfare of my family, and to act towards me and mine as you would have God act towards you and yours, and as I will act to you and yours if it please God that I survive you, and that your family have need of me.

It is said that when Gustavus presented the little girl to the Estates as his heir, tears came to the eyes of those northern men, who had the name of being cold and stern, as they repeated their oath of allegiance to the young princess.

"I know," the king said to them, "the perils, the fatigues, the difficulties of the undertaking, yet neither the wealth of the House of Austria dismays me nor her veteran forces. I hold my retreat secure under the worst alternative. And if it is the will of the Supreme Being that Gustavus should die in the defence of the faith, he pays the tribute with thankful acquiescence; for it is a king's duty and his religion to obey the great Sovereign of Kings without a murmur. For the prosperity of all my subjects I offer my warmest prayers to Heaven. I bid you all a sincere—it may be an eternal—farewell."

At this time he could hardly speak for emotion. He clasped his wife to him and said "God bless you! "and then, rushing forth, he mounted his horse and galloped down to the ship that was to take him away from Sweden.

Sweden was anything but rich, yet so inspired had the people become by the exalted spirit of their monarch, that they were eager to contribute whatever they could to the campaign.

On June 24, 1630, Gustavus was the first man of his expedition to land on the Island of Usedom, where he immediately seized a pickaxe and broke the soil for the first of his entrenchments. Then, retiring a little way from his officers, he fell upon his knees and prayed.

Observing a sneering expression upon the faces of some of his officers at this, he said to them: "A good Christian will never make a bad soldier. A man that has finished his prayers has at least completed one half of his daily work."

A painting commemorating this event is said still to be in existence in a Swedish country-house belonging to the family of de la Gardie.

Hardly a month after the landing of Gustavus Ferdinand deprived himself of his most able general; he removed Wallenstein,—the Duke of Friedland,—disbanding a large part of his army, and putting the rest under the command of Tilly, who now being over seventy, was slow in getting his army ready for the field.

When Ferdinand heard of the Swedish king's arrival on German soil, he had said lightly, "I have got another little enemy! "But by Christmas time Gustavus was established firmly on the banks of the Rhine, while ambassadors and princes surrounded him.

On reaching Stettin, in Pomerania, the king found his course opposed by Boguslas, the aged and infirm Duke of Pomerania, who feared to espouse the cause of the Protestant prince. But Gustavus insisted upon entering Stettin and seeing the duke. When the latter came to meet him, borne along the street on a sedan chair, he responded to Gustavus's hearty greetings by saying lugubriously, "I must necessarily submit to superior power and the will of Providence." At which Gustavus said with gracious pleasantry, that was no doubt trying to the timid old man, "Yonder fair defendants of your garrison "(the windows were crowded with ladies) "would not hold out three minutes against one company of Dalicarnian infantry; you should behave yourself with greater prowess in the married state" (the duke was over seventy and had no children) "or else permit me to request you to adopt me for your son and successor." This was a jest in earnest, for on the death of the duke the Swedes held possession of Pomerania, which was confirmed to them by subsequent treaty.

Germany was astounded at the orderly and moral behaviour of the Swedish soldiers; nothing save "vinegar and salt" were they allowed to make any demand for outside the camp. In January a notable event occurred. Richelieu, having in view the effect that so favourable a diversion would have on the war then going on in Italy between France and the House of Austria, had at last arranged conditions that Gustavus could accept.

Richelieu, as Wakeman says, "had long fixed his eyes on Gustavus as one of the most formidable weapons capable of being used against the House of Austria, and he desired to put it in the armoury of France."

In January, 1631, Gustavus signed the treaty of Barwalde, by which he undertook to maintain an army of thirty-six thousand men, to respect the Imperial Constitution, observe neutrality towards Bavaria and the Catholic League as they observed it towards him, and to leave the Catholic religion untouched in those districts where it was established. France was to supply the king with two hundred thousand dollars yearly for six years.

In March a great gathering of Protestants was held in Leipzig; they agreed to raise troops if they themselves were attacked, but they were willing to submit to the emperor if he would but repeal the Edict of Restitution. There seemed to have been some distrust of Gustavus among them; no doubt they began to fear already that he would prove too much of a conqueror.

There had been great sympathy in England with Gustavus in his character as a Protestant champion. Charles I. himself was quite indifferent, but his subjects, particularly his Scotch subjects, were anxious to be of service in the campaign.

In July of 1631 the Marquis of Hamilton had landed on the shores of the Baltic with six thousand troops, generously raised at his own expense. The marquis was a magnificent fellow, who lived in the field like a prince, with gorgeous liveries, equipages, and table. The king received him affectionately, but although he commanded his own troops he never achieved the rank of general in the Swedish army.

It is said that the English soldiers were not of great service in the war, and that they were fearfully affected by the strange food. The German bread gave them terrible pangs (it must have been Pumpernickel); they overfed themselves dreadfully with new honey, and the German beer played havoc with them. In this way the British contingent was soon reduced to but two regiments, finally to only one, and the Marquis of Hamilton was content to follow Gustavus as a simple volunteer.

An expostulating letter from Charles I. to Gustavus in relation to Hamilton is said to be almost unintelligible except for a postscript, which reads:

> I hope shortly you will be in a possibility to perform your promise concerning pictures and statues, therefore now in earnest do not forget it.

Gustavus Adolphus sent back to Scotland many well-trained commanders who had occasion afterwards to use their skill acquired under him. Some of these had a European reputation: Spence, of Warminster, created by Gustavus Count Orcholm; Alexander Leslie, afterwards Earl of Leven; Drummond, Governor of Pomerania; Lindsay, Earl of Crawford; Ramsay; Hepburn; Munro, and, most devoted and beloved of all the king's Scottish officers, Sir Patrick Ruthven.

Various squabbles have been recorded as taking place between the Scotchmen and the king. One relates to Colonel Seton, who was mortally offended at receiving a slap in the face from the king. He demanded instant dismissal from the Swedish service, and it was given him. He was riding off towards Denmark when the king overtook him.

"Seton," he said, "I see you are greatly offended with me, and I am sorry for what I did in haste. I have a high regard for you, and have followed you expressly to offer you all the satisfaction due to a brother officer. Here are two swords and two pistols; choose which weapon you please, and you shall avenge yourself against me."

This was too great an appeal to Seton's magnanimity; he broke out with renewed expressions of the utmost devotion to the king and his cause, and they rode back to camp together.

At one time Hepburn declared with fury to Gustavus that "he would never more unsheath his sword in the Swedish quarrel," but, nevertheless, he did do so, and was made Governor of Munich. The truth was that Gustavus had a domineering spirit and a fiery temper, but meanness or injustice had no part in him, and his noble candour won the true and everlasting attachment of those who were near him.

At one time Douglas, a Scotchman who had enrolled himself in the Swedish army in 1623, behaved in so unpardonable a fashion in Munich as to cause his arrest. Sir Henry Vane, the British ambassador to Sweden, who was greatly disliked there for his insolence and pig-headedness, approached Gustavus and demanded the release of Douglas.

"By Heaven!" replied the king, "if you speak another syllable on the subject of that man, I will order him to be hanged." Presently, however, he said: "I now release him on *your* parole, but will not be affronted a second time. By Heaven! the fellow is a rascal, and I do not choose to be served by such sort of animals."

"May it please your majesty, I have always understood that the subjects of the king my master have rendered you the most excellent and faithful services."

"Yes, I acknowledge the people of your nation have served me well, and far better than any others, but this dog concerning whom we are talking has affronted me, and I am resolved to chastise him." Within a few moments he had grown calmer, and said: "Sir, I request you not to take exception at what has dropped from me; it was the effect of a warm and hasty temper. I am now cool again, and beseech you to pardon me."

He once spoke of this temper to his generals, saying, "You must bear with my infirmities, as I have to bear with yours."

That Gustavus had so open a way before him this far in Germany, that he had been able to walk through Pomerania and Brandenburg without encountering any opposition that he could not easily overcome, was owing to Wallenstein's Imperial command having been taken from him.

One of the cleverest strokes Richelieu had ever made was the securing the dismissal of Wallenstein from the Imperial army. It seems a miraculous piece of craft, at the very moment when Wallenstein's arms had brought glorious victory to the emperor, and when Gustavus, absolute master of his military operations, was advancing on German soil, to deprive the Imperial armies of the only leader whose authority could stand against the great talents of Gustavus.

To be sure, there was great dissatisfaction with Wallenstein among the Catholic League on account of his personal pretensions, but this of itself would not have brought about his downfall. The only effectual voice to influence Ferdinand was the voice of a priest. His own confessor wrote of Ferdinand:

Nothing upon earth was more sacred to him than a sacerdotal head. If it should happen, he often said, that he were to meet, at the same time and place, an angel and a priest, the priest would obtain the first and the angel the second act of obeisance.

So Richelieu introduced in his court a gentle Capuchin monk, Father Joseph, who lived but to scheme for his master the cardinal. He told the emperor, among other arguments, that "It would be prudent at this time to yield to the desire of the princes the more easily to gain their suffrages for his son in the election of the King of the Romans. The storm once passed by, Wallenstein might quickly enough resume his former station."

Ferdinand piously gave in to the gentle monk, although he afterwards discovered the trickery; Wallenstein was removed and Tilly was made commander-in-chief.

Johann Tzerklas, Count von Tilly, was born in South Brabant in 1559, of an ancient and illustrious Belgian family. It is thought that he was educated for the Jesuit priesthood, and in this way became fanatically attached to Rome. At twenty-one he gave up the priesthood to enter the army of the Duke of Alva. Adopting the Imperial service, he followed the Duke of Lorraine into Hungary, where in some campaigns against the Turks he rose rapidly from one step to another.

At the conclusion of this war Maximilian of Bavaria made him commander-in-chief of his army with an unlimited power. When the unfortunate Elector Palatine Frederick accepted the crown of Bohemia and defied the emperor and his Catholic League, Maximilian took part with the emperor against him, and was rewarded, at the successful termination of the war, by having the Palatine countries given to him. The defeat of Frederick's forces in 1620 was no doubt due to Tilly's generalship. Poor Frederick, who fled from Tilly in terror and abdicated his electorate when he had two armies ready to support him, explained his poltroonery by saying philosophically: "I know now where I am; there are virtues which only misfortune can teach us; and it is in adversity alone that princes learn to know themselves."

Tilly, like Wallenstein, paid his troops on "the simple plan, that they shall get who have the power, and they shall keep who can."

But Tilly was undoubtedly more disinterested in his character than Wallenstein, who worked for his own aggrandisement, and only pretended to be at one time Protestant, at another Catholic.

Tilly was a sincere bigot, of the sort of stuff that the infamous Duke of Alva, whom he was said to resemble personally, was made. "A strange and terrific aspect," says Schiller in describing Tilly, "corresponded with this disposition: of low stature, meagre, with hollow cheeks, a long nose, a wrinkled forehead, large whiskers, and a sharp chin. He generally appeared dressed in a Spanish doublet of light green satin with open sleeves, and a small but high-crowned hat upon his head, which was ornamented with an ostrich-feather that reached down to his back."

This horrible fanatic, with his ferocious thirst for the blood of Protestants, nevertheless appreciated his adversary's powers: "The King of Sweden," he said in the assembly of the electors at Ratisbon, "is an enemy as prudent as brave; he is inured to war and in the prime of life; his measures are excellent, his resources extensive, and the states of his kingdom have shown him the greatest devotion. His army, composed of Swedes, Germans, Livonians, Finlanders, Scotch, and English, seems to be animated by but one sentiment, that of blind obedience to his commands. He is a gamester from whom much is won even when nothing is lost."

Tilly had no fondness for parade, and appeared among his troops mounted on a wretched little palfrey. By a curious contradiction, this man, who allowed his men to perform unspeakable acts of cruelty and lust, was himself by nature both temperate and chaste.

Field Marshal Tilly was now an old man, but he could boast that he had never lost a battle. Yet he who had vanquished Mansfield, Christian of Brunswick, the Margrave of Baden, and the King of Denmark, was now to find the King of Sweden too much for him.

The progress of the "Snow King" in Pomerania and Brandenburg made the new commander-in-chief put forth all his powers to collect the military forces scattered through Germany, but it was midwinter before he appeared with twenty thousand men before Frankfort-on-the-Oder. Here he had news that Demmin and Colberg had both surrendered to the King of Sweden, and, giving up his offensive plan of attack, he retired towards the Elbe River to besiege Magdeburg.

On his way, however, he turned aside to New Brandenburg, which Gustavus had garrisoned with two thousand Swedes, Germans, and British, and, angered by their obstinate resistance, put every man of them to the sword. When Gustavus heard of this massacre he vowed that he would make Tilly behave more like a person of humanity than a savage Croatian.

Breaking up his camp at Schwedt, he marched against Frankfort-on-the-Oder, which wets defended by eight thousand men—the same ferocious bands that had been devastating Pomerania and Brandenburg. The town was taken by storm after a three days' siege. Gustavus himself, helped by Hepburn and Lumsden, whom he asked to assist him with their "valiant Scots, and remember Brandenburg," placed a petard on a gate which sent it flying. The Swedish troops rushed through, and when the Imperial soldiers asked to be spared, they cried, "Brandenburg quarter!" and cut them down. Thousands were killed or drowned in the river. The remainder, excepting a number of officers who were taken prisoners, fled to Silesia. All the artillery fell into the hands of the Swedes. For the first time the king was unable wholly to restrain his men—all the stores of ill-gotten Imperialist wealth in Frankfort were grabbed by his army.

Giving Leslie charge of Frankfort, and having sent one detachment into Silesia, and another to assist Magdeburg, he then—turning aside, incidentally, to carry Landsberg-on-the-Warth—proceeded towards Berlin with troops and artillery, sending couriers in advance to explain his mission, which was to demand help from his brother-in-law, the elector.

The elector invited the king to dine and sleep at Berlin under the protection of his own guard, and consented to the temporary occupation of the fortresses of Spandau and Kustrin by the king's men, a permission which was withdrawn within a few weeks. When remonstrated with for these concessions the next day by one of his advisers, the elector said: *"Mais que faire? Us ont des canons."* It is a remark which seems to explain the lazy, inconsequent character of the elector, who, however, was always ready to admit the logic of superior force.

Magdeburg, one of the richest towns of Germany, enjoyed a republican liberty under its wise magistrates. The rich archbishopric of which it was the capital had belonged for a long period to the Protestant princes of the House of Brandenburg, who had introduced their religion there. The Emperor Ferdinand had removed the Protestant administration and given the archbishopric to his own son, Leopold, but, nevertheless, the city of Magdeburg had found it possible to conclude an alliance with the King of Sweden, by which he promised to protect with all his powers its religious and civil liberties, while he obtained permission to recruit in its territory and was granted free passage through its gates.

He sent there Dietrich, of Falkenberg, an experienced soldier, to direct their military operations, and the magistrates made him governor of the city during the war.

While Gustavus was hindered from coming to its relief, Magdeburg was invested by the forces of Tilly, with those of Count Pappenheim, who served under him. Having ordered the Elector of Saxony to comply with the Edict of Restitution and to order Magdeburg to surrender, and having received a firm refusal, Tilly proceeded, March 30, 1631, to conduct the siege personally with great vigour, and finally, after a long, heroic defence, his men carried it by storm May 20. Falkenberg was one of the first to fall. Then began the storied horrors of Magdeburg, the slaughter of the soldiers, the citizens, the children, the outrages and murder of the women, many of whom killed themselves to escape the demons let loose by Tilly.

Many Germans felt pity for the wretched women delivered into their hands, but the Walloons of Pappenheim's army were monsters of brutal fury. The scenes of crime in Magdeburg were unsurpassed in animal insanity by anything that has been recorded. When some officers of the League, sickened with these sights, appealed to Tilly to stop them, he said, "The soldier must have some reward for his danger and his labours."

The inhabitants themselves, it is said, set fire to the city in twelve different places, preferring to be buried under the walls to yielding; but some authorities say it was fired by Pappenheim. Only the Cathedral and fifty houses were left from the conflagration; the rest had gone to ruin, soot, and ashes.

At last, on May 23, Tilly walked through the ruined streets of the city. More than six thousand bodies had been thrown into the Elbe; a much greater number of living and dead had been consumed in the flames—altogether thirty thousand were killed.

On the 24th a *Te Deum* was chanted in the Cathedral by Tilly's orders, and he wrote to his emperor that since the taking of Troy and the destruction of Jerusalem no such victory had been seen. He then marched his men away through the Hartz Mountains, avoiding a meeting with Gustavus.

Great and bitter complaints arose in all quarters now against Gustavus for not succouring the city that depended upon him, and he was obliged to publish a justification of himself. The facts had been that the two Protestant Electors of Saxony and Brandenburg insisted, in the most cowardly spirit, upon preserving their neutrality, and would not allow the king's army to cross their territory. Had he done so in despite of them, his retreat might have been cut *off*. While the siege was in progress, however, Gustavus finally came to Berlin, and said to the pusillanimous elector: "I march towards Magdeburg not for my own advantage, but for that of the Protestants. If no person will assist me I will immediately retreat, offer an accommodation to the emperor, and return to Stockholm. I am certain that Ferdinand will grant me whatever peace I desire; but let Magdeburg fall, and the emperor will have nothing more to fear from me; then behold the fate that awaits you!"

The elector was frightened, but would not yield a free passage for the Swedes through his dominions, and insisted upon having Spandau given back to him, and while Gustavus was arguing the question with him the news came that Magdeburg had fallen.

The horrible fate of the city sent a shudder throughout Germany. On the strength of it Ferdinand began to make fresh exactions, clearing out more Protestant bishoprics and demanding more men and funds from the electors; but all this had the effect of opening the eyes of the members of the Protestant Union to their own foolishness in not supporting Gustavus, "and the liberties of Germany arose out of the ashes of Magdeburg," says Schiller.

It was now realised that within eight months the "Snow King "had made himself master of four cities, forts, and castles, and had cleared the whole country behind him to the shores of the Baltic—a territory one hundred and forty miles wide. But while other princes were changing their attitude, the Elector of Brandenburg remained obstinately, stupidly resolved on his own idea—he must have Spandau back; at last Gustavus ordered his commander to evacuate the fortress, but he declared that from that day his brother-in-law should be treated as his enemy.

To emphasise this, he brought his whole army before Berlin, and when the elector sent ambassadors to his camp he said to them: "I will not be worse treated than the emperor's generals. Your master has received them in his states, has furnished them with all necessaries, surrendered every place which they desired, and, notwithstanding so much complaisance, he has not been able to prevail upon them to treat his people with more humanity. All that I require from him is security, a moderate sum of money, and bread for my troops; in return for which I promise to protect his states and to keep the war at a distance from him. I must, however, insist upon these points, and my brother the elector must quickly decide whether he will accept me for his friend or his capital plunderer."

A report of this speech, together with pointing the cannon against the town, had the effect of clearing away the elector's doubts and sweetening his fraternal relations with Gustavus. Most amiably he concluded a treaty, in which he consented to pay thirty thousand dollars monthly to the king, to allow the fortress of Spandau to remain in his hands, and engaged to open Kustrin at all times to his troops.

This decisive union of the Elector of Brandenburg with the Swedes was soon followed by others. The Elector of Saxony, who had had two hundred of his villages burned by Tilly, now joined Gustavus eagerly. When Gustavus, in order to test the Saxon ruler, who had heretofore been so shifty, sent word that he would make no alliance with him unless he would deliver up the fortress of Wittenberg, surrender as a hostage his eldest son, give the Swedish troops three months' pay, and surrender up all traitors in his ministry, the elector replied: "Not only Wittenberg, but Torgau, all Saxony, shall be open to him; I will surrender the whole of my family to him as hostages; and if that be insufficient, I will even yield up myself to him. Hasten back, and tell him that I am ready to deliver up all the traitors he will name, to pay his army the money he desires, and to venture my life and property for the good cause."

The king, convinced of his sincerity, withdrew his severe conditions. "The mistrust," said he, "which they showed me when I wished to go to the aid of Magdeburg awakened mine; the present confidence of the elector merits an equal return from me. I am content if he will furnish my army with a month's whole pay, and I even hope to be able to indemnify him for this advance." The Landgrave of Hesse-Cassel also joined him. The Dukes of Mecklenburg and Pomerania were already his firm friends.

Shortly after these events the king summoned his allies to meet him at Torgau at a council of war, for Tilly had invested Leipzig with a large army, and was threatening it with the fate of Magdeburg. The council decided upon pursuing Tilly at once, the Saxon elector saying this vehemently. Gustavus had had a short respite from warlike labours; he had visited Pomerania in June, where great rejoicings had been held on his behalf, and where he was joined by his queen, Maria Eleonora (just a year after he had landed), who had come from Sweden with reinforcements of six thousand Swedes.

But, after all, war was the dominating thought always with Gustavus; soon he was at headquarters making active preparations for the next battle. Cust, in his *Lives of the Warriors of the Thirty Years' War,* says:

> The bridge of Wittenberg being in his hands, he had already issued orders to Horn and Baner to meet him at this place of rendezvous, about sixteen miles from thence; Colonel Hay had been directed to occupy Havelberg; while Banditzen was now directed to remain in charge of the camp at Werben. The king, however, with the delicacy of a man of honour and station, kept all his troops on the western bank of the Elbe, that he might leave the Saxon army encamped on the right bank until he obtained from the elector his authority in writing to cross the bridge.

The united Saxon and Swedish armies joined their forces on September 7, 1631, and came within sight of Tilly's forces near Breitenfeld, a small town four miles from Leipzig. The king's governor of Leipzig had surrendered to Tilly two days before, but the "old corporal," as Gustavus called him, had inflicted no outrages upon the town.

Gustavus pushed his men forward rapidly, leaving tents and baggage behind him in his camp, thinking his men might well sleep in the fields at this season of the year. On the evening before the action Gustavus called his generals to him, explained the plan of battle to them, and told them that "they were about to fight tomorrow troops of a different stamp from Polanders or Cossacks, to whom they had hitherto been opposed.

"Fellow-soldiers," he said, "I will not dissemble the danger of the crisis. You will have a day's work that will be worthy of you. It is not my temper to diminish the merit of veteran troops like the Imperialists, but I know my own officers well, and scorn the thought of deceiving them. Our numbers are perhaps inferior, but God is just; and remember Magdeburg."

After riding about through the ranks with the sanguine, light-hearted manner that always inspired courage in his men, he retired for a few hours' sleep in his coach. And here, the chroniclers say, he dreamed that he had a pugilistic encounter with Tilly and floored him.

Tilly was waiting for them next morning on the slope of a hill, with large woods behind him, and his artillery on an eminence. His men wore white ribbons in their hats and helmets, and the allies, or confederates, as they were called, sprigs of holly or oak. The Imperial army was stretched in a single line, having neither a second line nor a reserve.

Gustavus kept his own men well separated from his Saxon troops. The Saxons were upon and behind a hill with their guns, while his own men were in separate bodies, each under its own commander, but capable of being shifted or massed according to the will of Gustavus in an incredibly short space of time. This manner of making his battle-field a chess-board, on which only his hand controlled the moves, was at that time unknown. It has been said by experts that Gustavus's tactics on the day of Leipzig added more to the art of war than any that had been invented since the days of Julius Caesar.

A strong wind raged, blowing thick dust in the faces of the Swedes, and, as the battle proceeded, the smoke of the powder. As Gustavus moved his men to the attack in compact columns, in order to pass the Loderbach, Pappenheim, at the head of two thousand cuirassiers, plunged at them with violence. The king, clad in grey, with a green plume in his grey beaver hat, and mounted on his horse—of the sort called "flea-bitten,"—made a dash forward at the head of his cavalry, anxious to get the wind in his favour and to get his left flank out of range of a battery. Pappenheim, whose advance had been made without orders, received a volley from the musketeers that made him reel, and Baner at the head of the reserve cavalry, and Gustavus himself with the right wing, came on him with such impetus as to drive him fairly from the field.

Meanwhile on Tilly's extreme right Furstenberg threw himself on the Saxons; they had no such training as the king's old forces, and flew in a wild rout. The Elector of Saxony, who was in the rear, joining their flight with his body-guard, never stopped until he reached Eilenburg, where he consoled himself with deep draughts of beer, quite content to be out of the fray.

Gustavus witnessed the panic and flight of the Saxons,—from whom he had not expected too much,—and an officer he had summoned being shot dead in the saddle, the king took his place and cheered his men forward, crying *"Vivat! vivat!"*.

The enemy fell back before the vigour of this attack. At the same time the king discovered from the thick clouds of dust about him that some large body of troops was near; he was told they were Swedes, but they were not there in accordance with his plan of battle, so he galloped up close to them, and coming back quickly organised his troops to receive an attack. "They are Imperialists," he said. "I see the Burgundian cross on their ensigns." It was here that the two Scottish regiments under Hepburn and Munro first practised firing by platoons. This was so amazing to the veteran Cronenberg and his fine Walloon infantry that they retired with all speed.

At four o'clock the king took charge of his right wing, wheeled it suddenly to the left, dashed up to the heights where the Imperial artillery was placed, and, capturing it, turned the fire of their own guns on the enemy. Gustavus now swooped down upon Tilly's rear.

Caught between this cavalry attack at the rear and Horn's infantry in front, the Imperialists made a tough struggle. When the sun went down only six hundred men were left to close around Tilly and carry him from the field. With that exception the army had been destroyed. Seven thousand lay dead in the field; five thousand prisoners remained to take service with the victors, as the custom was at that time.

The king threw himself on his knees among the dead and wounded to offer up thanksgivings. He had the alarm-bells set ringing in all the villages round about to apprise the country of his victory. He encamped with his army in the deserted camp of the enemy. Almost all the baggage of the Imperialists fell into the hands of the conquerors. Hardly a soldier among the killed and wounded had less than ten ducats in his pocket or concealed within his girdle or saddle. Now that the battle was over the Elector of Saxony joined Gustavus in his camp at night. The king, who could be astutely diplomatic, gave him all the credit for having advised the battle and kept silent as to the Saxon troops. The elector, transported with joy at the issue of the day, promised to

Gustavus the Roman crown. Gustavus lost no time in dallying with the Roman crown, but made new plans for action. He left Leipzig to the elector and set forward for Merseburg, which, with Halle, at once surrendered.

Here he gave his army a rest of ten days, and many Protestant princes joined him in council.

The Battle of Lutzen

The Battle of Lutzen

From the day of Leipzig, Tilly's fortunes left him; his past victories were forgotten and execrations were heaped upon him. Though he was wounded, he went to work with all his old energy to form a new army, but the emperor expressly commanded that he should never again risk any decisive battle.

The glorious victory at Leipzig is said to have changed not only the world's opinion of Gustavus, but his own opinion of himself. He was now more confident; he took a bolder tone with his allies, a more imperious one with his enemies, and even more decision and greater speed marked his military movements, though nothing tyrannical or illiberal was seen in him.

The emperor and the Catholic League were dumfounded at the annihilation of Tilly. Richelieu was beginning to think his auxiliary too powerful; Louis XIII. even was heard to mutter, "It is time to put a limit to the progress of this Goth."

"Alone, without a rival," Schiller says, "he found himself now in the midst of Germany; nothing could arrest his course. His adversaries, the princes of the Catholic League, divided among themselves, led by different and contrary interests, acted without concert, and consequently without energy. Both statesman and general were united in the person of Gustavus. He was the only source from which all authority flowed: he alone was the soul of his party, the creator and executor of his military plans. Aided by all these advantages, at the head of such an army, endowed with a genius to profit by all these resources, conducted besides by principles of the wisest policy, it is not surprising that Gustavus Adolphus was irresistible. In not much more time than it would have taken another to make a tour of pleasure, with the sword in one hand and pardon in the other he was seen traversing Germany from one end to the other as a conqueror, lawgiver, and judge. As if he had been the legitimate sovereign, they brought him from all parts the keys of the towns and fortresses. No castle resisted him, no river stopped his victorious progress, and he often triumphed by the mere dread of his name."

Many of his advisers pressed Gustavus to attack Vienna, but after careful consideration he thought he would serve his cause best by marching straight into the heart of Germany on the Main and the Rhine.

Ten days after Leipzig the king reached Erfurt and ordered Duke William of Saxe-Weimar to take possession of the city. Proceeding through the Thuringian Forest, he reached Konigshofen Schweinfurt, which yielded to him, as did Wurzburg. Marienberg he was obliged to take by storm; a great store of treasure was here, as well as the money which the Elector of Bavaria had sent to Tilly for the purpose of replacing his shattered army.

Great quantities of provisions, corn, and wine fell into Swedish hands. A coffin filled with ducats was found, and as it was lifted the bottom gave way, and the soldiers began to help themselves to the coin in the presence of the king. "Oh, I see how it is," said he; "it is plain they must have it; let the rogues convert it to their own uses."

In truth, the character of the Swedish army was no longer beyond suspicion; the soldiers had become to some extent demoralised with their conquests; the cruelties and barbarities that they had suffered had forced upon them terrible reprisals, and the usage of looting was so universal that they could not be held back from it.

Tilly had by this time collected a new army out of the Palatinate and come back to Fulda, and here he tried to get the consent of Maximilian of Bavaria to engage Gustavus in battle again, but the duke was fearful of having another army wiped out, now the only one the Catholic League possessed, and refused him.

The Swedish king now advanced rapidly towards the Rhine by way of the Main, reducing Aschaffenburg, Seligenstadt, and the whole territory on both sides of the river. The Count of Hanau made but slight resistance when his citadel was captured, and gladly agreed to pay two thousand five hundred pounds a month for the support of the army and to recall his retainers from the Imperial service.

Nothing now kept Gustavus from marching on Frankfort-on-the-Main. The magistrates of the city begged the ambassador that he sent to entreat him to consider their legitimate oaths to the emperor, and to leave them neutral, on account of their annual fairs, which were their chief commercial enterprise. The king was not moved by these touching business considerations; he was surprised, he replied, that while the liberties of Germany were at stake and the Protestant religion in jeopardy, they should convey to his ear such an odious sentiment as neutrality, and that the citizens of Frankfort should talk of annual fairs, as if they regarded all things merely as tradesmen and merchants, rather than as men of the world with a Christian conscience. More sternly he went on to say that he had found the keys to many a town and fortress from the Isle of Rugen on the Baltic to the banks of the Main, and knew well where to find a key for Frankfort.

The magistrates were filled with alarm at this, and asked for time to consult the Elector of Mayence, their ecclesiastic sovereign, but the king replied that he was master of Aschaffenburg; he was Elector of Mayence; he would give them plenary absolution.

"The inhabitants," he said, "might desire to stretch out only their little finger to him, but he would be content with nothing but the whole hand, that he might have sufficient to grasp."

He then moved his army on Saxenhausen, a beautiful suburb of the city, and here the magistrates met him, and after taking the oath of fidelity opened the gates of the city to him. The king made a solemn public entrance into the city, leading his troops with uncovered head, as a mark of respect, and bringing in fifty-six pieces of artillery. He was welcomed by the magistracy to a great banquet in the coronation hall of the imperial palace of Braunfels. Maria Eleonora, his queen, now joined him in Frankfort, and when she met him was so overcome with joy that, throwing her arms around him, she cried, "Now is Gustavus the Great become my prisoner!"

The next event of importance in this victorious progress was the carrying of Mayence, which after a short siege capitulated on December 13. On the 14th the king celebrated his thirty-seventh birthday by entering Mayence with great pomp, and took up his residence in the palace of the elector, ordering a service of thanksgiving for his success to be held in the Roman Catholic Cathedral. Provisions, artillery, and money fell into the hands of the army. The king seized as his personal share the library of the elector, and gave it to Oxenstiern for one of the Swedish universities, but, alas! it was lost in the Baltic.

The exhausted Swedish soldiers were now allowed a space of rest to recuperate their energies. On January 10 the queen arrived in Mayence and shared with Gustavus for a short time the ceremonial splendours of a regal court, where five German princes and many foreign ambassadors had come to confer with the king and transact important negotiations with him. Among these was the Marquis de Breze, an ambassador from the French court. By his conversation Gustavus detected something of the truth, that Richelieu now feared him and was trying to undermine his power.

Accordingly, he sent word to Louis XIII. that he wished to speak with him personally. The French ambassador tried to persuade Gustavus that an interview with Richelieu would do as well, but he replied haughtily: "All kings are equal. My predecessors have never given place to the kings of France. If your master thinks fit to despatch the cardinal half way, I will send some of my people to treat with him, but I will admit of no superiority."

When the king and queen left Mayence in mid-February, Gustavus had had a new citadel built at the confluence of the Rhine and Main, which was called at first "Gustavusburg," but in after days lapsed into "Pfaffenraube "(Priest-plunder). A lion of marble on a high marble pillar is near Mayence, holding a naked sword in his paw and wearing a helmet on his head, to mark the spot where the "Lion of the North "crossed the great river of Germany. During February Kreutznach in the Palatinate, one of the strongest castles in Germany, and the town of Ulm surrendered to the king.

Leaving Oxenstiern, his minister and friend, to protect his conquests on the Rhine and Main, Gustavus began his advance against the enemy March 4, 1632, with an army— including his allies' forces—of one hundred thousand infantry and forty thousand cavalry under arms. The Catholic League had been extremely active during the months since the defeat of Tilly at Breitenfeld and Leipzig, and had raised even larger forces.

By the capture of Donauworth it was evident to Tilly that Gustavus's next move was to be towards Bavaria, for he was now master of the right bank of the Danube. Accordingly, after destroying all the bridges in the vicinity, Tilly entrenched himself in a strong position on the other side of the river Lech. Numerous garrisons defended the river as far as Augsburg. The Bavarian elector shut himself up in Tilly's camp, feeling that the issue of the coming battle must decide everything for him.

The Lech, in the month of March, is swollen to a great torrent by the melting snows from the Tyrol, and dashes furiously between high, steep banks. The officers of Gustavus considered it impossible to effect a crossing and urged him not to try it. But he exclaimed to Horn—

"What! Have we crossed the Baltic and so many great rivers of Germany, and shall we now for this Lech, this rivulet, abandon our enterprise!"

He had made the discovery that his side of the river was higher by eleven feet than the opposite bank, which would greatly favour his cannon. He immediately took advantage of this by having three batteries erected on the spot where the left bank of the Lech forms an angle opposite its right. Here seventy-two pieces kept up a constant cannonade on the enemy.

He had now to invent a bridge that would cross the torrent, and also think of means to distract the enemy from noticing its construction. He made a strong set of trestles of various heights and with unequal feet, so that they would stand upright on the uneven bed of the river; these were secured in their places by strong piles driven into the river-bed. Planks were then nailed to the trestles. While this went on, the cannonade drowned the noise of the hammers and hatchets; one thousand musketeers lined the Swedish bank and kept the Imperialist soldiers from coming near enough to discover the work, while a thick smoke, made by burning wood and wet straw, hid the workmen for the most part.

Before daybreak the bridge was finished, and an army of engineers and soldiers selected by the king soon crossed it and threw up a substantial breastwork.

Tilly saw his foes entrenched on his own side of the river and, under the tremendous firing of the guns from the higher bank, was utterly powerless to keep them from coming. For thirty-six hours the cannonade went on, the king standing most of the time at the foot of the bridge and sometimes acting as gunner himself to encourage his men. The Imperialists made a desperate effort to seize the bridge, but a large number were cut down in the attempt.

Finally, Tilly, whose courage was heroic throughout the day, fell with a shattered thigh, and had to be borne away. Maximilian, the Bavarian duke, now precipitately abandoned his impregnable position and moved the army quietly away to Ingolstadt.

When Gustavus next day found the camp vacant his astonishment was great.

"Had I been the sovereign of Bavaria," he cried, "never, though a cannon-ball had taken away my beard and chin—never would I have quitted a post like this and laid my states open to the enemy."

Bavaria, indeed, lay open to the conqueror; before occupying it, however, he rescued the Protestant town of Augsburg from the Bavarian yoke, Augsburg being in his eyes a special object of veneration on account of the famous "Confession "—the place "from whence the law first proceeded from Sion." Augsburg, indeed, at first resisted him, but when he saw the dread devastation that his guns began to make on its beautiful buildings he stopped them and insisted on an interview with the governor, who, seeing the hopelessness of resistance, yielded.

Tilly died in Ingolstadt, the Elector of Bavaria sitting by his bedside. He adjured Maximilian to keep Ingolstadt with all his powers against Gustavus and to seize Ratisbon at once, begged him never to break his alliance with the emperor, and besought him to appoint General Gratz in his place. "He will conduct your troops with reputation, and, as he knows Wallenstein, will traverse the designs of that insolent man. Oh," he sighed, "would that I had expired at Leipzig and not survived my fame!"

So died Tilly—bigoted, merciless, cruel, but nevertheless faithful and zealous to his last breath in defence of his religion and the League.

Ingolstadt was a fortress considered impregnable; it had never been conquered. Gustavus had determined to take it, and made a partial investment only, for on one side of it was the whole Bavarian army under Maximilian.

While riding about the walls one day and going very near to take observations, on account of his short sight, a twenty-four pounder killed his horse—the favourite "flea-bitten" steed—under him; he rose tranquilly and, mounting another horse, continued his reconnoitring. In camp in the evening his generals in a body protested against his risking so valuable a life in this way; but he replied that he had a foolish sort of a fancy which always tempted him to imagine that he could see better for himself than others could, and that his sense of God's providence gave him the firm assurance that he had other assistance in store for so just a cause than the precarious existence of one Gustavus Adolphus.

Within a few days news came that the Bavarian troops had taken the Imperial town of Ratisbon, and this caused a change in the king's plans; he had spent eight days on Ingolstadt, but he now suddenly abandoned it, because it would have been of no special advantage to him without Ratisbon in his scheme of cutting off Maximilian from Bohemia.

Munich was his next objective point, and he now proceeded into the interior of Bavaria, where Mosburg, Landshut, all the Bishopric of Freysingen, surrendered to him. But the Bavarians looked upon Protestants as children of hell. Soldiers who did not believe in the Pope were to them accursed monsters. When they succeeded in capturing a Swedish straggler they put him to death with tortures the most refined and prolonged. When the Swedish army came upon mutilated bodies of their comrades they took vengeance into their own hands, but never by consent of Gustavus.

His approach to Munich threw the capital into an agony of terror. It had no defenders, and they feared that the treatment his soldiers had met at the hands of the country-people might lead him to use his power cruelly. Some Germans in his army begged to be allowed to repeat here the sacking of Magdeburg, but such a low revenge was impossible to the king. When the magistracy sent to implore his clemency, he answered that if they submitted readily and with good grace, care should be taken that no man should suffer with respect to life, liberty, or religion. Only one act of questionable taste accompanied his public entry, and that was the presence of a monkey in the procession—a monkey with a shaven crown and in a Capuchin's dress, with a rosary in his paw. One hopes that the king was not responsible for this.

He found an abandoned palace: the elector's treasures had been removed. There were left, though, many fine canvases by Flemish and Italian masters. His officers urged the king to plunder or destroy these, but he said: "Let us not imitate our ancestors, the Goths and Vandals, who destroyed everything belonging to the fine arts, which has left our nation a proverb and a byword of contempt with posterity for acts of this wanton barbarity." He had evidently forgotten the earnest request of Charles I. for "pictures and statues."

The construction of the palace—a magnificent building—caused the king to express great admiration: he asked the steward the name of the architect. "He is no other than the elector himself" was the reply. "I should like to have this architect," replied the king, "to send him to Stockholm." "That," said the steward, "he will take care to avoid."

The guns in the arsenal had been buried so carefully that they would not have been discovered if it had not been for a treacherous insider, who told the secret. "Arise from the dead," cried the king, "and come to judgment!" and one hundred and forty pieces of artillery were dug up, a large sum of gold being found in one of them.

Appointing the Scotchman Hepburn to the post of Governor of Munich, Gustavus soon started forth with his army.

Meanwhile Maximilian, although besought by his Bavarians to come and deliver them from the Swedes, could not resolve to risk a battle. The wonderful victories of Gustavus had indeed a paralysing effect upon the country. As yet no one had been found capable of resisting him. Richelieu himself was horror-stricken at the power he had helped to raise. It was expected in France that an invasion of Swedes would be the natural continuation of the Rhine conquests; it was said that Gustavus would not rest until he had made Protestantism compulsory throughout Europe.. Nothing less than the command of the German Empire was supposed to be his ultimate aim.

There is no doubt that his ambitions steadily enlarged themselves, but there is nothing to prove that he contemplated supplanting Ferdinand. His enemies were disheartened. Ferdinand was now brought to the pass of abjectly begging Wallenstein to resume his command, and Wallenstein was assuming airs of indifference and allowing himself to be persuaded only with great pressure.

This extraordinary man was the son of a Moravian baron of the ancient race of Waldstein. As a youth he was notably proud and stubborn, ambitious and conceited, often saying, "If I am not a prince, I may become one." He fell from a very high window whilst at the University of Goldben and was quite unhurt, which is said to have been the beginning of his certainty of future greatness. He was grossly superstitious always and entirely an egotist. At twenty-three he married a wealthy widow, who in a fit of jealousy gave him a "love philtre" in his wine, from which he narrowly escaped death. Dying in 1614, she left him a large property, and later he married a Countess Isabelle von Haggard, of immense fortune and of much "beauty, piety, and virtue."

Wallenstein now began to invest his great wealth in the purchase of confiscated properties, and it was said that through his knowledge of metallurgy he adulterated the coin which he paid. At all events, his wealth assumed fabulous dimensions, and through his wife's relations he mingled with the highest nobles of the empire. He always spoke with affection of his wife, but did not live with her nor write to her for years at a time.

In person Wallenstein was very tall and thin, with a yellow complexion, short red hair, and small, twinkling eyes. His cold, malignant gaze frightened his great troop of servants, who nevertheless stayed with him because they were unusually well paid. His military career had begun in his youth, when he served in Hungary.

Afterwards he raised a body of horse at his own expense for a war against the Venetians. On the breaking out of the war in Bohemia, in 1618, he was offered the post of general to the Bohemian forces, but adopted the side of the sovereign in whose family he had been brought up.

After putting down the Bohemian rebellion, in which Tilly had served Maximilian, the emperor decided that it was necessary for him to have a powerful army under his own orders. Wallenstein offered to raise an army, clothe, feed, and arm it at his own expense, if he should be made a field-general, an offer which the emperor accepted and which Wallenstein carried out.

His military activities from this time on are historical, as well as the details of his cold, pompous nature. He lived like a king, with great state, had no principles whatever about the way he acquired wealth, and spent it with magnificent lavishness.

At the time Ferdinand deprived him of his command, just as Gustavus was entering Germany, Wallenstein had become Duke of Friedland, Sagan, Glogau, and Mecklenburg, and was more insolent than if he had had royal blood in his veins. He spent an income of three millions of florins yearly, for his armies had plundered the land for years with great effect. He was able to control his rage at his sudden downfall because his Italian astrologer, Seni, who ruled him completely, assured him that the stars showed that a brilliant future awaited him, exalted beyond anything he had yet known. And so he was led on to close his career by plots against his emperor and to meet death by the hands of assassins.

All of Gustavus's successes were the source of deep satisfaction to Wallenstein; they brought nearer his inevitable recall.

Now when Tilly was dead, and the emperor was beseeching him again to take command of the Imperial troops, Wallenstein sent an envoy to convey the congratulations of the Duke of Friedland to the King of Sweden, and to invite his majesty to a close alliance with him. He undertook, in concert with Gustavus, to conquer Bohemia and Moravia and drive the emperor out of Germany.

Gustavus felt that help would be very welcome, and he seriously considered the offer; but he could not bring himself to believe in a success promised by such an unscrupulous adventurer, who so willingly offered to become a traitor. He courteously refused, and Wallenstein accepted the emperor's offer of chief command with a salary amounting to the value of one hundred and eight thousand pounds per annum. He demanded that he should have uncontrolled command of the German armies of Austria and Spain, with unlimited power to reward and punish. Neither the King of Hungary (to whom the emperor had wished to give the highest command) nor the emperor himself was ever to appear in his army or exercise the slightest authority in it. No commission or pension was to be granted without Wallenstein's approval. An Imperial hereditary estate in Austria was to be assigned to him. As the reward of success in the field he should be made lord paramount over the conquered countries, and all conquests and confiscations should be placed entirely at his disposal. All means and moneys for carrying on the war must be solely at his command.

The ambassador to whom he made these terms suggested that the emperor must have some control over his armies, and that the young King of Hungary should at least be allowed to study the art of war with Wallenstein, but the reply was: "Never will I submit to any colleague in my office; no, not even if it were God Himself with whom I should have to share my command." In his extremity the emperor accepted these conditions, April 15, 1632.

Although an avowed Jesuit, Wallenstein had no religious scruples whatever, and the Catholics feared and hated him as much as the Protestants. The gorgeous luxury of his surroundings was apparently only designed to impress the world; -he was not a sensualist, but seems to have been actuated only by an insane love of power. Soldiers flocked to his standard and worshipped the mighty warrior who rewarded them with ceaseless plunder, but the princes, nobles, and peasantry of the countries through which he passed were left with a blight upon them. He seemed to be unable to see in a country any reasons for industrial prosperity or for conserving wholesome conditions of any sort; he was a brave, fearless leader—after that, a robber, and nothing else.

He distributed enormous sums among his favourites, and the amount he spent in corrupting the members of the Imperial Court was still greater. The height to which he raised the Imperial authority astonished even the emperor; but his design unquestionably was, that his sovereign should stand in fear of no one in all Germany besides himself, the source and engine of his despotic power. He cared nothing, however, himself, for popularity from his equals, and less for the detestation of the people or the complaints of the sovereigns, but was ready to bid a general defiance to all consequences.

Wallenstein raised his army. From Italy, Scotland, Ireland, as well as from every part of Germany, men flocked to him in thousands who cared little for country or religion, but were attracted by the prospects of plunder and of distinction under the renowned soldier who had made himself a dictator.

In May, 1632, his organisation was complete. He began by driving Gustavus's Saxon allies out of Bohemia, while Pappenheim scourged the Rhine country. Then he directed his forces upon rich Protestant Nuremberg.

Gustavus, before he could get there, threw himself into Nuremberg and fortified it, and then, gathering his army together, prepared to give battle to Wallenstein. But the latter had made up his mind to starve out Gustavus. With his own light cavalry, superior in number to that of the Swedes, he could more readily obtain supplies than they.

Forming a huge camp on an eminence overlooking Nuremberg, he prepared stolidly to wait until the king should be forced to go. At the end of June the camp was finished, and Gustavus held out until September.

His men were starving and dying, discipline had become relaxed, even his generals becoming cruel and rapacious. On September 3 he had led his men against Wallenstein's entrenchments, but was forced to retire. A few days later he left Nuremberg, providing it with a garrison, although he had lost through battle, disease, and starvation nearly twenty thousand men. Wallenstein's loss in the same time was thirty-six thousand. No attempt at pursuit was made by Wallenstein. Turning north into Saxony, he proceeded to choose a position between the Elbe and the Saale, where he might entrench himself for the winter and carry on what to him was one of the most necessary features of a campaign—the sending of bands of marauders and requisitioners through the country.

He also had in mind detaching the Saxon elector from his alliance with Gustavus, this vacillating prince having shown symptoms of yielding to the great furore caused by Wallenstein's resumption of power.

Gustavus determined that he should not lose Saxony by want of decision. Summoning Oxenstiern and Bernhard of Saxe-Weimar to his aid, he forced his army with all speed through Thuringia, and before Wallenstein could recover from his astonishment he seized both Erfurt and Naumburg.

At Erfurt he said farewell to his queen, who never saw his face again until he was in his coffin at Weissenfels.

The weather had become so bitterly cold that Wallenstein had expected no further advances from Gustavus during the winter. He was preparing to entrench himself between Merseburg and Torgau. He had sent Pappenheim again to the Rhineland. Gustavus took advantage of this division and resolved to fight before Pappenheim could return to reinforce his adversary. Wallenstein sent messenger after messenger to bring back Pappenheim, and hastily throwing up entrenchments, he awaited the onslaught of the Swedish king at the village of Lutzen, November 6.

On the southern side of the large highway leading from Lutzen to Leipzig lay the Swedes; to the north, the Imperialists. Two ditches ran by the sides of this road, and some old willow-trees bordered it. The deep, rich mould of the soil is heavy for horse and foot. On Wallenstein's right was a hill where a group of windmills waved their arms.

On the evening of the 5th the Duke of Friedland had ordered his men to deepen and widen the ditches, and he planted two large batteries on the windmill hill. Gustavus had passed the night in his coach with the Duke of Saxe-Weimar, for he owned neither tent nor field equipage. He had ordered his army to be ready two hours before daylight, but there was so solid a fog that the darkness was intense, and not a step could be taken. Gustavus had his chaplain perform divine service while waiting. He never forgot, it was said, either the time to pray or the time to pay—never leaving his men's wages in arrears. He would take no breakfast and declined to put on his steel breastplate, as a wound he had received made it uncomfortable. He was clad in a new plain cloth doublet and an elk-skin *surtout*.

Riding along the ranks, he encouraged each regiment, addressing Swedes and Germans in their respective tongues, and urging all to valour and steadfastness. "God with us!"

was the rallying-cry of the Swedes. *"Jesu Maria!"* was the shout of the Imperialists.

The morning wore on, as the soldiers waited still in impenetrable darkness. At one time Gustavus threw himself on his knees and began a hymn, the military band accompanying him. His terrible weeks at Nuremberg and the hardships of the late toilsome march had seemed to bring out more strongly than ever the fervent piety of his nature. When, on his arrival a few days before at Naumburg, the people had rushed from all the country round to see him, and had prayed on their knees for the favour of touching the hem of his garment or his sword in its scabbard, he was touched by this innocent worship, but he was moved to say to those with him: "Does it not seem as if this people would deify me? Our affairs go on well without doubt, but I much fear that Divine vengeance will punish me for this rash mockery, and soon convince the foolish multitude of my weak mortality."

Towards eleven o'clock the fog began to lighten, and the enemies could see each other, while the Swedes beheld the flames of Lutzen, set on fire by Wallenstein that he might not be flanked on that side.

Gustavus now mounted his horse and drew his sword for action, placing himself at the head of the right wing. Wallenstein opened the attack with a tremendous fire of musketry and artillery, with which Gustavus's leather guns found it hard to cope. The ditches of the road made a formidable obstacle to the Swedish cavalry, being lined with musketeers. But at length the Swedish musketeers cleared the others away. The horsemen, however, under the heavy firing, now seemed to find the ditches impassable; they hesitated before them, whereupon Gustavus dashed forward to lead them across.

"If," said he sternly, "after having passed so many rivers, scaled so many walls, and fought so many battles, your old courage fails you, stand still but for a moment and see your master die in the manner we all ought to be ready to do."

He leaped the ditch, and they were after him like the wind, urging him to spare his invaluable life and promising to do everything. On the other side of the road and ditches he observed three dark masses of Imperial cuirassiers clad in iron, and turning to a colonel said: "Charge me those black fellows, for they are men that will undo us; as for the Croats, I mind them not."

The royal order was at once executed, but the Croats suddenly swept down upon the Swedish baggage and actually reached the king's coach, which, however, they failed to capture.

Both sides fought desperately; it had to be decided whether it was Gustavus's genius that had won at the battle of the Lech and at Leipzig, or if Tilly's want of skill had been the only cause. On this day Wallenstein, Duke of Friedland, had to justify the emperor's confidence and the enormous demands he had made upon it. Each soldier of each side seemed to feel that the honour and success of his chieftain depended solely on his individual efforts.

The Swedes advanced with such velocity and force that the first, second, and third Imperial brigades were forced to fly; but Wallenstein stopped the fugitives. Supported by three ranks of cavalry, the beaten brigades formed a new front to the Swedes and struck furiously into their ranks. A murderous series of combats then began; there was no space for even loading muskets—they fought wildly with sword and pike. At last the Swedes, exhausted, withdrew to the other side of the ditches, abandoning a battery they had gained.

In the meantime the king, at the head of his right wing, had attacked the enemy's left. His splendidly powerful cuirassiers of Finland had easily routed all the Croats and Poles covering this wing, and their flight spread confusion among the rest of the cavalry. But he then received the news that his infantry had retired, and that his left wing, under the heavy fire of the windmill hill, was about to yield.

Ordering Horn to pursue the wing which he had just defeated, he turned to fly to the assistance of his own men. His horse carried him so swiftly that no one kept up with him but the Duke of Lauenburg.

He galloped straight to the place where his men were being assailed with the greatest fury, and his near-sightedness led him too near. An Imperialist corporal noticed that all gave way before him with great respect, and shouted to a musketeer: "Fire at him! That must be a man of distinction!" and the king's left arm was shattered.

He begged Lauenburg to help him to a place of safety, but the next moment he was shot in the back. Turning to Lauenburg he said: "Brother, I have enough; seek only to save your own life."

As he spoke he fell to the ground, where a volley of other shots pierced him.

A desperate struggle still took place over him. A German page, refusing to tell the royal rank of his master, was mortally shot. But Gustavus still had life enough to say: "I am the King of Sweden, and seal with my blood the Protestant religion and the liberties of Germany." Then he murmured: "My God! Alas! my poor queen!"

For a long time the Duke of Lauenburg was accused of assassinating the king, and there is a great deal to be said in support of such a charge. Among the Spanish archives were found papers showing that there was a plot in progress to kill Gustavus. Still, it is conceivable that his death was caused by the ordinary chances of war.

It was the king's charger, galloping into the Swedish lines covered with blood, that brought the news of the king's death. The Swedish cavalry came with furious speed to the place to rescue the precious remains of their king. A great conflict raged around his dead body until it was heaped with the slain. The dreadful news, spreading through the Swedish army, inflamed their courage to desperation; neither life nor death mattered to them now; the Yellow Guard of the king was nearly cut to pieces.

Bernhard, Duke of Weimar, a warrior of great skill and courage, took command of the army. The Swedish regiments under General Horn completely defeated the enemy's left wing, took possession of the windmill hill, and turned Wallenstein's cannon against him. The Swedish centre advanced and carried the battery again, and while the enemy's resistance grew more feeble, their powder-wagons blew up with fearful roars. Their courage seemed to give way, and victory was assured to the Swedes.

Then Pappenheim arrived at the head of his cuirassiers and dragoons, and there was a new battle to fight. This unexpected reinforcement renewed and fired the courage of the Imperialists. Wallenstein seized the favourable moment to form his lines again. Again he drove the Swedes back and recaptured his battery. Every man of the Yellow Regiment, which had most distinguished itself on the side of the Swedish infantry, lay dead in the order in which he had fought.

The Blue Regiment also had been blotted out by a terrific charge of the Austrian horse under Count Piccolomini, who had, during the charge, seven horses shot under him, and was hit in six places. While the worst of the conflict was going on, Wallenstein rode through it with cold intrepidity; men and horses fell thick around him and his mantle was full of bullet-holes, but he escaped unhurt.

Pappenheim was wounded in the thigh, and the next moment a musket-ball tore his chest. He felt that he had got his death-blow, but was able to speak cheerfully to his men, who carried him away in his coach to Leipzig. He was replaced by Hoik.

Duke Bernhard re-formed his men, and the fight went on with a stubborn fury that nothing could assuage. Neither side would be beaten. Again and again the Swedes were forced back; again and again they rallied and drove back their antagonists.

Ten leaders on each side had fallen. The Imperial side finally weakened with the loss of its generals. At nightfall the Swedes formed all their broken regiments into one dense mass, made their final movement across the ditches, captured the battery, and turned its guns on the enemy.

Confused as the Imperialists had become, they still fought. The bloody struggle went on until it was too dark to see anything; both armies then left the field, each claiming the victory. Pappenheim's army left their guns, being without a general and having no orders. It was said that after Pappenheim was borne away Wallenstein betook himself to a sedan chair and did not again expose himself to the enemy. He was reproached for this afterwards by his army, who also said that he retired from the field before it was necessary. Proceeding to Leipzig, he witnessed the death of Pappenheim. Piccolomini was the last of his side in the field.

The Duke of Friedland insisted on having the Te Deum sung in honour of a victory in the churches, but this deceived no one. It was no victory, but a defeat from which he never recovered. While at Leipzig he accused his officers of cowardice, and after a court-martial had several of the bravest of them disgraced or shot. But neither this nor a few inconsequent successes were sufficient to restore the prestige that Wallenstein had lost at Lutzen.

Nearly one hundred thousand corpses remained unburied on the field, and the plain all around was covered with wounded and dying.

It was not until the next day that the Swedes were able to find the body of their king; it was almost unrecognisable with blood and wounds, trampled by horses' hoofs, and naked. A huge stone was rolled by the soldiers as near as they could to the place where the royal corpse was found; it still rests where they left it, and is known as "The Stone of the Swede."

The Imperialists had stripped the body in their eagerness to preserve relics of the great Gustavus. Piccolomini sent his buff waistcoat to the emperor. His rings, spurs, and gold chain are still in possession of various families. A famous turquoise is supposed to have passed into the hands of a Roman Catholic bishop who desired a trophy of "Anti-Christ," as Gustavus was called by the Catholics.

The body was carried from the field in solemn state amid a procession of the whole army. It was taken to Weissenfels, and from thence to Sweden. There the whole nation mourned, knowing well that they should not have another monarch like Gustavus Adolphus.

Nothing has ever transpired to change the world's opinion of him as one of the world's greatest and best. Although the Thirty Years' War was not concluded for several years after his death, yet he was, nevertheless, the cause of its cessation. Through his agency alone the cause of the Protestant belief triumphed, and the effects of the great upheaval of the Reformation were not allowed to be obliterated in Germany.

Professor Smyth said of him: "It is fortunate when the high courage and activity of which the human character is capable are tempered with a sense of justice, wisdom, and benevolence; when he who leads thousands to the field has sensibility enough to feel the responsibility of his awful trust, and wisdom enough to take care that he directs against its proper objects alone the afflicting storm of human devastation. It is not always that the great and high endowments of courage and sagacity are so united with other high qualities as to present to the historian at once a Christian, a soldier, and a statesman. Yet such was Gustavus Adolphus, a hero deserving of the name, perfectly distinguishable from those who have assumed the honours that belong to it—the mere military executioners with whom every age has been infested."

Cust says:

Gustavus Adolphus is thought to have been the first sovereign who set the example of a standing army. The feudal association of barons with their retainers had given way in the previous century to a set of military adventurers, who made war a profession to gratify their license and their acquisitiveness, and who were commissioned by kings and leaders to collect together the assassins of Europe.

These constituted at the very time of the Thirty Years' War the unprincipled and insatiate legions who harried Germany, who, without much discipline, were continually dissipated by the first disaster and collected together again, as it were from the four winds of heaven, to cover the face of the land again and again with terror, devastation, and confusion.

Gustavus, who had witnessed this from afar, or experienced it in his Polish wars, had in him that spirit of organisation and order which signally distinguished him above every great leader who preceded him. He saw that a well-disciplined force of men to be commanded by a superior class of officers of high honour and intelligence, and who should constitute an armed body that might obtain the dignity of a profession of arms, would be more efficient and a cheaper defence of nations than the haphazard assembling of mere bloodhounds, and he first executed the project of having a force of eighty thousand men, part in activity and part in reserve, who should be constantly maintained well-armed, well-clothed, well-fed, and well-disciplined.

The Storming
of Badajoz

IN THE BREACH AT BADAJOZ

The Storming of Badajoz

In studying the campaign in the Peninsula, one must remember first of all that the man who was made Earl of Wellington for the victory at Ciudad Rodrigo was not the great potentiality who, as the Duke of Wellington, influenced England after Waterloo. During the Peninsula campaign Wellington was afflicted at all times by a bitter and suspicious Parliament at home. They had no faith in him, and they strenuously objected to furnishing him with money and supplies. Wellington worked with his hands tied behind him against the eager and confident armies of France. We ourselves can read in our more frank annals how a disgruntled part of Congress was for ever wishing to turn Washington out of his position as head of the colonial forces.

Parliament doled supplies to Wellington with so niggardly a hand that again and again he was forced to stop operations for the want of provisions and arms. At one time he actually had been told to send home the transports in order to save the expense of keeping them at Lisbon. The warfare in Parliament was not deadly, but it was more acrimonious than the warfare in the Peninsula. Moreover, the assistance to his arms from Portugal was so wavering, uncertain, and dubious that he could place no faith in it. The French marshals, Soult and Marmont, had a force of nearly one hundred thousand men.

Wellington held Lisbon, but if he wished to move in Portugal there always frowned upon him the fortified city of Badajoz. But finally there came his chance to take it, if it could be taken in a rush, while Soult and Marmont were widely separated and Badajoz was left in a very confident isolation.

Badajoz lies in Spain, five miles from the Portuguese frontier. It was the key of a situation. Wellington's chance was to strike at Badajoz before the two

French marshals could combine and crush him. His task was both in front of him and behind him. He lacked transport; he lacked food for the men; the soldiers were eating cassava root instead of bread; the bullocks were weak and emaciated. All this was the doings of the Parliament at home. But Wellington knew that the moment to strike had come, and he seems to have hesitated very little. Placing no faith in the tongues of the Portuguese, he made his plans with all possible secrecy. 9 The guns for the siege were loaded on board the transports at Lisbon and consigned to a fictitious address. But in the river Sadao they were placed upon smaller vessels, and finally they were again landed "and drawn by bullocks to Eloas, a post in the possession of the allies. Having stationed two-thirds of his force under General Graham and General Hill to prevent a most probable interference by Soult and Marmont, Wellington advanced, reaching Eloas on the nth of March 1812. He had made the most incredible exertions. The stupidity of the Portuguese had vied with the stupidity of the government at home. Wellington had been carrying the preparation for the campaign upon his own shoulders. If he was to win Badajoz, he was to win it with no help save that from gallant and trustworthy subordinates. He was ill with it. Even his strangely steel-like nature had bent beneath the trouble of preparation amid such indifference. But on March 16 Beresford with three divisions crossed the Guadiana on pontoons and flying bridges, drove in the enemy's outposts, and invested Badajoz.

At the time of the investment the garrison was composed of five thousand French, Hessians, and Spaniards. Spain had always considered this city a most important barrier against any attack through Portugal. A Moorish castle stood three hundred feet above the level of the plain. Bastions and fortresses enwrapped the town. Even the Cathedral was bombproof. The Guadiana was crossed by a magnificent bridge, and on the farther shore the head of this bridge was strongly fortified.

Wellington's troops encamped to the east of the town. It was finally decided first to attack the bastion of Trinidad. The French commander had strengthened all his defences, and by damming a stream had seriously obstructed Wellington's operations. Parts of his force were confronted by an artificial lake two hundred yards in width.

The red coats of the English soldiers were now faded to the yellow brown of fox fur. All the military finery of the beginning of the century was tarnished and torn. But it was an exceedingly hard-bitten army, certain of its leaders, despising the enemy, full of ferocious desire for battle.

Perhaps the bastion of Trinidad was chosen because it was the nearest to the entrenchments of the allies. In those days the frontal attack was possible of success. On the night of the 17th of March the British broke ground within one hundred and sixty yards of Fort Picerina. The sound of the digging was muffled by the roar of a great equinoctial storm. The French were only made wise by the daylight, but in the meantime the allies had completed a trench six hundred yards long and three feet deep, and with a communication four thousand feet in length. The French announced their discovery by a rattle of musketry, but the allies kept on with their digging, while general officers wrapped in their long cloaks paced to and fro directing the work.

The situation did not please the French general at all. He knew that something must be done to counteract the activity of the besiegers. He was in command of a very spirited garrison. On the night of the 19th a sortie was made from the Talavera Gate by both cavalry and infantry. The infantry began to demolish the trench of the allies. The cavalry divided itself into two parts and went through a form of sham fight, which in the darkness was deceptive. When challenged by the pickets, they answered in Portuguese, and thus succeeded in galloping a long way behind the trenches, where they cut down a number of men before their identity was discovered and they were beaten back. General Phillipon, the French commander, had offered a reward for every captured entrenching tool. Thus the French infantry of the sortie devoted itself largely to making a collection of picks and spades. Men must have risked themselves with great audacity for this reward, since they left three hundred dead on the field, but succeeded in carrying off a great number of the entrenching tools.

Great rain-storms now began to complicate the work of the besiegers. The trenches became mere ditches half full of discoloured water. This condition was partly improved by throwing in bags of sand. On the French side a curious device had been employed as a means of communication between the gate of the Trinidad bastion and Fort San Roque. The French soldiers had begun to dig, but had grown tired, so they finished by hanging up a brown cloth. This to the besiegers' eyes was precisely like the fresh earth of a parallel, and behind it the French soldiers passed in safety.

Storm followed storm. The Guadiana, swollen past all tradition by these furious downpours, swept away the flying bridges, sinking twelve pontoons. For several days the army of the allies was entirely without food, but they stuck doggedly to their trenches, and when communication was at last restored it was never again broken. The weather cleared, and the army turned grimly with renewed resolution to the business of taking Badajoz. This was in the days of the forlorn hope. There was no question of anything but a desperate and deadly frontal attack. The command of the assault of Fort Picerina was given to General Kempt. He had five hundred men, including engineers, sappers, and miners, and fifty men who carried axes. At nine o'clock they marched. The night was very dark. The fort remained silent until the assailants were close. Then a great fire blazed out at them. For a time it was impossible for the men to make any progress. The palisades seemed insurmountable, and the determined soldiers of England were falling on all sides. In the meantime there suddenly sounded the loud, wild notes of the alarm-bells in the besieged city, and the guns of Badajoz awakened and gave back thunder for thunder to the batteries of the allies. The confusion was worse than in the mad nights on the heath in *King Lear,* but amid the thundering and the death, Kempt's fifty men with axes walked deliberately around Fort Picerina until they found the entrance gate. They beat it down and rushed in. The infantry with their bayonets followed closely. Lieutenant Nixon of the Fifty-second Foot (now the Second Battalion of the Oxfordshire Light Infantry) fell almost on the threshold, but his men ran on. The interior of the fort became the scene of a terrible hand-to-hand fight. All of the English did not come in through the gate. Some of Kempt's men now succeeded in establishing ladders against the rampart, and swarmed over to the help of their comrades. The struggle did not cease until more than half of the little garrison were killed. Then the commandant, Gasper Thiery, surrendered a little remnant of eighty-six men. Others who had not been killed by the British had rushed out and been drowned in the waters of that inundation which had so troubled Wellington and so pleased the French general. Phillipon had estimated that the Picerina would endure for five days, but it had been taken in an hour, albeit one of the bloodiest hours in the annals of a modern army.

Wellington was greatly pleased. He was now able to advance his earthworks close to the eastern part of the town, while his batteries played continually on the front of Fort San Roque and the two northern bastions, Trinidad and Santa Maria.

But at the last of the month Wellington was confronted by his chief fear. News came to him that Marshal Soult was advancing rapidly from Cordova. It was now a simple question of pushing the siege with every ounce of energy contained in his army. Forty-eight guns were made to fire incessantly, and although the French reply was destructive, the English guns were gradually wearing away the three great defences. By the 2nd of April Trinidad was seriously damaged, and one flank of Santa Maria was so far gone that Phillipon set his men at work on an inner defence to cut the last-named bastion off from the city. On the night of the 2nd an attack was made on the dam of the inundation. Two British officers and some sappers succeeded in gagging and binding the sentinel guarding the dam, and having piled barrels of gunpowder against it, they lighted a slow-match and made off. But before the spark could reach the powder the French arrived under the shelter of the comic brown cloth communication. The explosion did not occur, and the inundation still remained to hinder Wellington's progress. On the 6th it was thought that three breaches were practicable for assault, and the resolute English general ordered the attack to be made at once. To Picton, destined to attach his name to the imperishable fame of Waterloo, was given an arduous task. He was to attack on the right and scale the walls of the castle of Badajoz, which were from eighteen to twenty-four feet high. On the left General Walker, marching to the south, was to make a false attack on Port Pardaleras, but a real one on San Vincente, a bastion on the extreme west of the town. In the centre the Fourth Division and Wellington's favourite Light Division were to march against the breaches. The Fourth was to move against Trinidad, and the Light Division against Santa Maria. The columns were divided into storming and firing parties. The former were to enter the ditch while the latter fired over them at the enemy. Just before the assault was to be sounded a French deserter brought the intelligence that there was but one communication from the castle to the town, and Wellington decided to send against it an entire division. Brigadier-General Power with his semi-useless Portuguese brigade was directed to attack the head of the bridge and the other works on the right of the Guadiana.

The army had now waited only for the night. When it had come, thick mists from the river increased the darkness. At 10 o'clock Major Wilson, of the Forty-eighth Foot (now the First Battalion of the Northamptonshire regiment), led a party against Fort San Roque so suddenly and so tempestuously that the work capitulated almost immediately. At the castle, General Picton's men had placed their ladders and swarmed up them in the face of showers of heavy stones, logs of wood, and crashing bullets, while at the same time they were under a heavy fire from the left flank. The foremost were bayoneted when they reached the top, and the besieged Frenchmen grasped the ladders and tumbled them over with their load of men. The air was full of wild screams as the English fell towards the stones below. Presently every ladder was thrown back, and for the moment the assailants had to run for shelter against a rain of flying missiles.

In this moment of uncertainty one man, Lieutenant Ridge, rushed out, rallying his company. Seizing one of the abandoned ladders, he planted it where the wall was lower. His ladder was followed by other ladders, and The troops scrambled with revived courage after this new and intrepid leader. The British gained a strong foothold on the ramparts of the castle, and every moment added to their strength as Picton's men came swarming. They drove the French through the castle and out of the gates. They met a heavy reinforcement of the French, but after a severe engagement they were finally and triumphantly in possession of the castle. Lieutenant Ridge had been killed.

But at about the same time the men of the Fourth Division and of the Light Division had played a great and tragic part in the storming of Badajoz. They moved against the great breach in stealthy silence. All was dark and quiet as they reached the glacis. They hurled bags full of hay in the ditch, placed their ladders, and the storming parties of the Light Division, five hundred men in all, hurried to this desperate attack.

But the French general had perfectly understood that the main attacks would be made at his three breaches, and he had made the great breach the most impregnable part of his line. The English troops, certain that they had surprised the enemy, were suddenly exposed by dozens of brilliant lights. Above them they could see the ramparts crowded with the French. These fire-balls made such a vivid picture that the besieged and besiegers could gaze upon one another's faces at distances which amounted to nothing. There was a moment of this brilliance, and then a terrific explosion shattered the air. Hundreds of shells and powder-barrels went off together, and the English already in the ditch were literally blown to pieces. Still their comrades crowded after them with no definite hesitation. The French commander had taken the precaution to fill part of the ditch with water from the inundation, and in it one hundred fusiliers, men of Albuera, were drowned.

The Fourth Division and the Light Division continued the attack upon the breach. Across the top of it was a row of sword-blades fitted into ponderous planks, and these planks, chained together, were let deep into the ground. In front of them the slope was covered with loose planks studded with sharp iron points. The English, stepping on them, rolled howling backward, and the French yelled and fired unceasingly.

It was too late for the English to become aware of the hopelessness of their undertaking. Column after column hurled themselves forward. Young Colonel Macleod, of the Forty-third Foot (now the First Battalion of the Oxfordshire Light Infantry), a mere delicate boy, gathered his men again and again and led them at the breach. A falling soldier behind him plunged a bayonet in his back, but still he kept on till he was shot dead within a yard of the line of sword-blades.

For two hours the besiegers were tirelessly striving to achieve the impossible, while the French taunted them from the ramparts.

"Why do you not come into Badajoz?"

Meanwhile, Captain Nicholas of the Engineers, with Lieutenant Shaw and about one hundred men of the Forty-third Foot, actually had passed through the breach of the Santa Maria bastion, but once inside they were met with such a fire that nearly every man dropped dead. Shaw returned almost alone.

Wellington, who had listened to these desperate assaults and watched them as well as he was able from a position on a small knoll, gave orders at midnight for the troops to retire and re-form. Two thousand men had been slain. Dead and mangled bodies were piled in heaps at the entrance to the great breach, and the stench of burning flesh and hair was said to be insupportable.

And still, in the meantime, General Walker's brigade had made a feint against Pardaleras and passed on to the bastion of San Vincente. Here for a time everything went wrong. The fire of the French was frightfully accurate and concentrated. General Walker himself simply dripped blood; he was a mass of wounds. His ladders were all found to be too short. The walls of the fortress were thirty feet in height. However, through some lack of staying power in the French, success at last crowned the attack. One man clambered somehow to the top of a wall and pulled up others, until about half of the Fourth Foot (now the King's Own Royal Lancaster Regiment) were fairly into the town. Walker's men took three bastions. General Picton, severely wounded, had not dared to risk losing the Castle, but now, hearing the tumult of Walker's success, he sent his men forth and thousands went swarming through the town. Phillipon saw that all was lost, and retreated with a few hundred men to San Christoval. He surrendered next morning to Lord Fitzroy Somerset.

The English now occupied the town. With their comrades lying stark, or perhaps in frightful torment, in the fields beyond the walls of Badajoz, these soldiers, who had so heroically won this immortal victory, became the most abandoned drunken wretches and maniacs. Crazed privates stood at the corners of streets and shot every one in sight. Everywhere were soldiers dressed in the garb of monks, of gentlemen at court, or mayhap wound about with gorgeous ribbons and laces. Jewels and plate, silks and satins, all suffered a wanton destruction. Napier writes of "shameless rapacity, brutal intemperance, savage lust, cruelty and murder, shrieks and piteous lamentations."

He further says that the horrible tumult was never quelled. It subsided through the weariness of the soldiers. One wishes to inquire why the man who was ultimately called the Iron Duke did not try to stop this shocking business. But one remembers that Wellington was a wise man, and he did not try to stop this shocking business because he knew that his soldiers were out of control, and that if he tried he would fail.

The Battle of
New Orleans

THE BATTLE OF NEW ORLEANS

The Battle of New Orleans

The Mississippi, broad, rapid, and sinister, ceaselessly flog-
ging its enwearied banks, was the last great legend of the
dreaming times when the Old World's information of the
arisen continents was roseate but inaccurate. England, at war
with the United States, heard stories of golden sands, bejew-
elled temples, fabulous silks, the splendour of a majestic bar-
barian civilisation; and even if these tales were fantastic they
stood well enough as symbols of the spinal importance of the
grim Father of Waters.

The English put together a great expedition. It was the
most formidable that ever had been directed against the
Americans. It assembled in a Jamaican harbour and at Pensa-
cola, then a Spanish port and technically neutral. The troops
numbered about fourteen thousand men and included some
of the best regiments in the British army, fresh from service in
the Peninsula under Wellington. They were certainly not men
who had formed a habit of being beaten. Included in the expedition was a full set of civilian officials for the government
of New Orleans after its capture.

A hundred and ten miles from the mouth of the Mississippi, New Orleans lay trembling. She had no forts or entrenchments; she would be at the mercy of the powerful British force.
The people believed that the city would be sacked and burned.
They were not altogether a race full of vigour. The peril of the
situation bewildered them; it did not stir them to action.

But the spirit of energy itself arrived in the person of Andrew Jackson. Since the Creek War, the nation had had much confidence in Jackson, and New Orleans welcomed him with a great sigh of relief. The sallow, gnarled, crusty man came ill to his great work; he should have been in bed. But the amount of vim he worked into a rather flabby community in a short time looked like a miracle. The militia of Louisiana were called out; the free negroes were armed and drilled; convicts whose terms had nearly expired were enlisted; and down from Tennessee tramped the type of man that one always pictures as winning the battle—the long, lank woodsman, brown as leather, hard as nails, inseparable from his rifle, in his head the eye of a hawk.

The Lafitte brothers, famous pirates, whose stronghold was not a thousand miles from the city, threw in their lot with the Americans. The British bid for their services, but either the British committed the indiscretion of not bidding enough or the buccaneers were men of sentiment. At any rate they accepted the American pledge of immunity and came with their men to the American side, where they rendered great service. Afterwards the English, their offer of treasure repulsed, somewhat severely reproved us for allowing these men to serve in our ranks.

Martial law was proclaimed, and Jackson kept up an exciting quarrel with the city authorities at the same time that he was working his strange army night and day in the trenches. Captain John Coffee with two thousand men joined from Mobile.

The British war-ships first attempted to cross the sand-bars at the mouth of the river and ascend the stream, but the swift Mississippi came to meet them, and it was as if this monster, immeasurable in power, knew that he must defend himself. The well-handled warships could not dodge this simple strength; even the wind refused its help. The river won the first action.

But if the British could not ascend the stream, they could destroy the small American gunboats on the lakes below the city, and this they did on December 14 with a rather painful thoroughness. The British were then free to land their troops on the shores of these lakes and attempt to approach the city through miles of dismal and sweating swamps. The decisive word seems to have rested with Major-General Keane. Sir George Pakenham, the commander-in-chief, had not yet arrived. One of Wellington's proud veterans was not likely to endure any nonsensical delay over such a business as this campaign against a simple people who had not had the art of war hammered into their heads by a Napoleon. Moreover, the army was impatient. Some of the troops had been with Lord Ross in the taking of Washington, and they predicted something easier than that very easy campaign. Everybody was completely cocksure.

On the afternoon of December 23, Major-General Gabrielle Villere, one of the gaudy Creole soldiers, came to see Jackson at headquarters, and announced that about two thousand British had landed on the Villere plantation, nine miles below the city. Jackson was still feeble, but this news warmed the old passion in him. He pounded the table with his fist. "By the Eternal!" he cried, "they shall not sleep on our soil! "All well-regulated authorities make Jackson use this phrase—" By the Eternal!"—and any reference to him hardly would be intelligible unless one quoted the familiar line. I suppose we should not haggle over the matter; historically one oath is as good as another.

Marching orders were issued to the troops, and the armed schooner *Carolina* was ordered to drop down the river and open fire upon the British at 7.50 in the evening. In the meantime, Jackson reviewed his troops as they took the road. He was not a good-natured man; indeed, he is one of the most irascible figures in history. But he knew how to speak straight as a stick to the common man. Each corps received some special word of advice and encouragement.

This review was quaint. Some of the Creole officers were

very gorgeous, but perhaps they only served to emphasise the wildly unmilitary aspect of the procession generally. But the woodsmen were there with their rifles, and if the British had beaten Napoleon's marshals, the woodsmen had conquered the forests and the mountains, and they too did not understand that they could be whipped.

The first detachment of British troops had come by boat through Lake Borgne and then made a wretched march through the swamps. Both officers and men were in sorry plight. They had been exposed for days to the fury of tropical rains, and for nights to bitter frosts, without gaining even an opportunity to dry their clothes. But December 23 was a clear day lit by a mildly warm sun. Arriving at Villere's plantation on the river bank, the troops built huge fires and then raided the country as far as they dared, gathering a great treasure of "fowls and hams and wine." The feast was merry. The veteran soldier of that day had a grand stomach, and he made a deep inroad into Louisiana's store of "fowls and hams and wine."

As they lay comfortably about their fires in the evening some sharp eye detected by the faint light of the moon a moving shadowy vessel on the river. She was approaching. An officer mounted the levee and hailed her. There was no answer. He hailed again. The silent vessel calmly furled her sails and swung her broadside parallel. Then a voice shouted, and a whistling shower of grape-shot tore the air. It was the little *Carolina*.

The British forces flattened themselves in the shelter of the levee and listened to the grape-shot go ploughing over their heads. But they had not been long in this awkward position when there was a yell and a blare of flame in the darkness. Some of Jackson's troops had come.

Then ensued a strange conflict. The moon, tender lady of the night, hid while around the dying fires two forces of infuriated men shot, stabbed, and cut. One remembers grimly Jackson's sentence—"They shall not sleep on our soil." No; they were kept awake this night at least.

There was no concerted action on either side. An officer gathered a handful of men and by his voice led them through the darkness at the enemy. If such valour and ferocity had been introduced into the insipid campaigns of the North, the introduction would have made overwhelming victory for one people or the other. Dawn displayed the terrors of the fighting in the night. In some cases an American and an English soldier lay dead, each with his bayonet sheathed in the other's body.

Bayonets were rare in the American ranks, but many men carried long hunting knives.

As a matter of fact, the two forces had been locked in a blind and desperate embrace. The British reported a loss of forty-six killed, one hundred and sixty-seven wounded, and sixty-four missing. In this engagement the Americans suffered more severely than in any other action of the short campaign.

On the morning of December 24, Sir George Pakenham arrived with a strong reinforcement of men and guns. Pakenham was a brother-in-law of Wellington. He had served in the Peninsula and was accounted a fine leader. The American schooners *Carolina* and *Louisiana* lay at anchor in the river firing continually upon the British camp. Pakenham caused a battery to be planted which quickly made short work of these vessels.

During the days following the two armies met in several encounters which were fiery but indecisive. One of these meetings is called the Battle of the Bales and Hogsheads.

Jackson employed cotton-bales in strengthening a position, and one night the British advanced and built a redoubt chiefly of hogsheads containing sugar and molasses. The cotton suffered considerably from the British artillery, often igniting and capable of being easily rolled out of place, but the sugar and molasses behaved very badly. The hogsheads were easily penetrated, and they soon began to distribute sugar and molasses over the luckless warriors in the redoubt, so that British soldiers died while mingling their blood with molasses, and with sugar sprinkling down upon their wounds.

Although neither side had gained a particular advantage, the British were obliged to retire. They had been the first disciplined troops to engage molasses, and they were glad to emerge from the redoubt, this bedraggled, sticky, and astonished body of men.

On the opposite bank of the river a battery to rake the British encampment had been placed by Commander Patterson. This battery caused Pakenham much annoyance, and he engaged it severely with his guns, but at the end of an hour he had to cease firing with a loss of seventy men and his emplacements almost in ruins. The damage to the American works was slight, but they had lost thirty-six in killed and disabled.

Both sides now came to a period of fateful thought. In the beginning the British had spoken of a feeble people who at first would offer a resistance of pretence, but soon subside before the victorious colours of the British regiments. Now they knew that they were face to face with determined and skilful fighters who would dauntlessly front any British regiment whose colours had ever hung in glory in a cathedral of old England. The Americans had thought to sweep the British into the Gulf of Mexico. But now they knew that although their foes floundered and blundered,—although they displayed that curious stern-lipped stupidity which is the puzzle of many nations,—they were still the veterans of the Peninsula, the stout, undismayed troops of Wellington.

Jackson moved his line fifty yards back from his cotton-bale position. Here he built a defensive work on the northern brink of an old saw-mill race known as the Rodriguez Canal. The line of defence was a mile in length. It began on the river bank and ended in a swamp where, during the battle, the Americans stood knee-deep in mud or on floating planks and logs moored to the trees. The main defences of the position were built of earth, logs, and fence-rails in some places twenty feet thick. It barred the way to New Orleans.

The Americans were prepared for the critical engagement some days before Pakenham had completed his arrangements. The Americans spent the interval in making grape-shot out of bar-lead, and in mending whatever points in their line needed care and work.

Pakenham's final plan was surprisingly simple, and perhaps it was surprisingly bad. He decided to send a heavy force across the river to attack Patterson's annoying battery simultaneously with the deliverance of the main attack against Jackson's position along the line of the Rodriguez Canal. Why Pakenham decided to make the two attacks simultaneously is not quite clear at this day. Patterson's force, divided by the brutally swift river from the main body of the Americans, might have been considered with much reason a detached body of troops, and Pakenham might have eaten them at his leisure while at the same time keeping up a great show in front of Jackson, so that the latter would consider that something serious was imminent at the main position.

However, Pakenham elected to make the two attacks at the same hour, and posterity does not perform a graceful office when it re-generals the battles of the past.

Boats were brought from the fleet, and with immense labour a canal was dug from Lake Borgne to the Mississippi. For use in fording the ditch in front of Jackson, the troops made fascines by binding together sheaves of sugar-cane, and for the breastwork on the far-side of the ditch they made scaling ladders.

On January 7, 1815, Jackson stood on the top of the tallest building within his lines and watched the British at work. At the same time Pakenham was in the top of a pine-tree regarding the American trenches. For the moment, and indefinitely, it was a question of eyesight. Jackson studied much of the force that was to assail him; Pakenham studied the position which he had decided to attack. Pakenham's eyesight may not have been very good.

Colonel Thornton was in command of the troops which were to attack Patterson's battery across the river, and a rocket was to be sent up to tell him when to begin his part of the general onslaught.

Pakenham advanced serenely against the Rodriguez Canal, the breastwork, and the American troops. One wishes to use here a phrase inimical to military phraseology. One wishes to make a distinction between disinterested troops and troops who are interested. The Americans were interested troops. They faced the enemy at the main gate of the United States. Behind them crouched frightened thousands. In reality they were defending a continent.

As the British advanced to the attack they made a gallant martial picture. The motley army of American planters, woodsmen, free negroes, ex-convicts, and pirates watched them in silence. Here tossed the bonnets of a fierce battalion of Highlanders; here marched a bottle-green regiment, the officers wearing furred cloaks and crimson sashes; here was a steady line of blazing red coats. Everywhere rode the general officers in their cocked hats, their short red coats with golden epaulettes and embroideries, their skin-tight white breeches, their high black boots. The ranks were kept locked in the manner of that day. It was like a grand review.

But the grandeur was extremely brief. The force was well within range of the American guns when Pakenham made the terrible discovery that his orders had been neglected: there was neither fascine nor ladder on the field. In a storm of rage and grief the British general turned to the guilty officer and bade him take his men back and fetch them. When, however, the ladders and fascines had been brought into the field, a hot infantry engagement had already begun, and the bearers, becoming wildly rattled, scattered them on the ground.

It was now that Sir George Pakenham displayed that quality of his nation which in another place I have called stern-lipped stupidity. It was an absolute certainty that Jackson's position could not be carried without the help of fascines and ladders; it was doubtful if it could be carried in any case.

But Sir George Pakenham ordered a general charge. His troops responded desperately. They flung themselves forward in the face of a storm of bullets aimed usually with deadly precision. Back of their rampart, the Americans, at once furious and cool, shot with the quickness of aim and yet with the finished accuracy of life-long hunters. The British army was being mauled and mangled out of all resemblance to the force that had landed in December.

Sir George Pakenham, proud, heartbroken, frenzied man, rode full tilt at the head of rush after rush. And his men followed him to their death. On the right, a major and a lieutenant succeeded in crossing the ditch. The two officers mounted the breastwork, but the major fell immediately. The lieutenant imperiously demanded the swords of the American officers present. But they said, "Look behind you." He looked behind him and saw that the men whom he had supposed were at his back had all vanished as if the earth had yawned for them.

The lieutenant was taken prisoner and so he does not count, but the dead body of the major as it fell and rolled within the American breastwork established the high-water mark of the British advance upon New Orleans.

Sir George Pakenham seemed to be asking for death, and presently it came to him. His body was carried from the field. General Gibbs was mortally wounded. General Kean'e was seriously wounded. Left without leaders, the British troops began a retreat. This retreat was soon a mad runaway, but General Lambert with a strong reserve stepped between the beaten battalions and their foes. The battle had lasted twenty-five minutes.

Jackson's force, armed and unarmed, was four thousand two hundred and sixty-four. During the whole campaign he lost three hundred and thirty-three. In the final action he lost four killed, thirteen wounded. The British force in action was about eight thousand men. The British lost some nine hundred killed, fourteen hundred wounded, and five hundred prisoners.

Thornton finally succeeded in reaching and capturing the battery on the other side of the river, but he was too late. Some of the British war-ships finally succeeded in crossing the bars, but they were too. late. General Lambert, now in command, decided to withdraw, and the expedition sailed away.

Peace had been signed at Ghent on December 24, 1814. The real battle of New Orleans was fought on January 8, 1815.

The Battle of Solferino

CARRYING THE CEMETERY GATE AT SOLFERINO

The Battle of Solferino

"Italy," said Prince Metternich, "is merely a geographical expression."

The sneer was justified; the storied peninsula was cut up into little principalities for little princes of the houses of Hapsburg and Bourbon. The millions who spoke a common tongue and cherished common traditions of a glorious past were ruled as cynically as if they were so many cattle. The map of Italy for 1859 is a crazy-quilt of many patches. How has it come about, then, that the map of Italy for 1863 is of one uniform colour from the Alps to the "toe of the boot," including Sardinia and Sicily? We must except the Papal States, of course, still separate till 1870, and Venetia, Austrian till 1866, when the "Bride of the Sea" became finally one with the rest of Italy.

This was the last miracle that Europe had looked for. Unity in Italy! "Since the fall of the Roman Empire (if ever before it)," said an Englishman, "there has never been a time when Italy could be called a nation any more than a stack of timber can be called a ship." This was true even in the days of the mediaeval magnificence of the city-states, Venice, Genoa, Milan and Florence, Pisa and Rome. But in modern times Italy had become only a field for intriguing dynasties and the wars of jealous nations.

During the latter half of the eighteenth century Italy was strangely tranquil, Was she content at last with her slavery? Never that; the people had simply grown apathetic. Their spasmodic insurrections had always ended in a worse bondage than ever: their very religion was used to fasten their chains. Perhaps nothing could have served so well to wake them from this torpor of despair as the iron tread of the first Napoleon. The "Corsican tyrant" proved a beneficent counter-irritant—a wholesome, cleansing force throughout the land. It was good for Italy to be rid, if only for a little while, of Hapsburgs and Bourbons; to have the political divisions of the country reduced to three; to be amazed at the sight of justice administered fairly and taxation made equitable. But the most significant effect of the Napoleonic occupation was this, that the hearts of the Italians were stirred with a new consciousness: they had been shown the possibility of becoming a united race—of owning a nation which should not be a "mere geographical expression."

And although 1815 brought the bad days of the Restoration, and the stupid, corrupt, or cruel princes climbed back again on their little thrones, and the map was made into pretty much the same old crazy-quilt, still it was not the same old Italy: all the diplomats at Vienna could not make things as they had been before. The new spirit of freedom came to life in the north, in the kingdom of Sardinia, that had made itself the most independent section of the country. In the beginning it was only Savoy, and the Dukes of Savoy, "owing," as the Prince de Ligne said, "to their geographical position, which did not permit them to behave like honest men," had swallowed, first, Piedmont; then, Sardinia; and then as many of the towns of Lombardy as they could. The restoration enriched the kingdom by the gift of Genoa, where, in 1806, Joseph Mazzini was born.

Mazzini, Garibaldi, Cavour—those names will be always thought of as one with the liberation of Italy.

Though frequently in open antagonism, yet the work of each of the three was necessary to the cause, and to each it was a holy cause, for which he was ready to make any sacrifice:

Italia! when thy name was but a name, When to desire thee was a vain desire, When to achieve thee was impossible, When to love thee was madness, when to live For thee was the extravagance of fools, When to die for thee was to fling away Life for a shadow—in those darkest days Were some who never swerved, who lived, and strove, And suffered for thee, and attained their end.

Of these devoted ones Mazzini was the prophet; his idealism undoubtedly made

too great demands upon the human beings he worked for, but let us bear in mind that it needed a conception of absolute good to rouse the sluggish Italian mind from its materialism and Machiavellism. Mazzini wore black when a youth as "mourning for his country," and when his university course was at an end he took up the profession of political agitator and joined the Carbonari.

But the greatest service he ever did his cause was the organisation of a new society—on a much higher plane than the Carbonari and its like. The movement was called "Young Italy," famous for the spirit it raised from end to end of the peninsula. Among those attracted by Mazzini's exalted utterance was the young Garibaldi, who, taking part in Mazzini's rising of 1834, was condemned to death, and made his escape to South America. In constant service in the wars between the quarrelsome states he gained his masterly skill in guerrilla warfare, which was afterwards to play so great a part in the liberation of his country. He did not return until it seemed as though the hour of Italy's deliverance was at hand, in 1848, which only proved to be the "quite undress rehearsal" for the great events of 1859.

Garibaldi has been called "not a soldier but a saint." Most great heroes, alas! have outlived their heroism, and their worshippers have outlived their worship; but Garibaldi has never been anything but the unselfish patriot who wanted everything for his country but nothing for himself. He has been described, on his return to Italy from South America, as "beautiful as a statue and riding like a centaur."

"He was quite a show," said the sculptor Gibson, "every one stopping to look at him."

"Probably," said another Englishman, "a human face so like a lion, and still retaining the humanity nearest the image of its Maker, was never seen."

The third of the immortal Italian trio, Count Camillo de Cavour, was, like Mazzini and Garibaldi, a subject of the Sardinian kingdom. There was no prouder aristocracy in Europe than that of Piedmont, but Camillo seems to have drawn his social theories from the all-pervading unrest that the great Revolution and Bonaparte had left in the air, rather than the assumed sources of heredity. In his tenth year he entered the military academy at Turin, and at the same time was appointed page to the Prince of Carignan, afterwards Charles Albert, father of Victor Emmanuel. This was esteemed a high honour, but it did not appeal to him in this light. When asked what was the costume of the pages, he replied, in a tone of disgust: "Parbleu! how would you have us dressed, except as lackeys, which we were? It made me blush with shame."

His attitude of contempt for the place occasioned a prompt dismissal. At the academy he was so successful with mathematics that he left it at sixteen, having become sub-lieutenant in the engineers, although twenty years was the earliest age for this grade. He then joined the garrison at Genoa, but the military career had no allurements for him. Taking kindly to liberal ideas, he expressed himself so freely that the authorities transferred him to the little fortress of Bard, till, in 1831, he resigned his commission.

Having by nature a "diabolical activity" that demanded the widest scope for itself, he now took charge of a family estate at Leri, and went in for scientific farming.

"At the first blush," he wrote, "agriculture has little attraction. The habitué of the salon feels a certain repugnance for works which begin by the analysis of dunghills and end in the middle of cattle-sheds. However, he will soon discover a growing interest, and that which most repelled him will not be long in having for him a charm which he never so much as expected."

Although he began by not knowing a turnip from a potato, his invincible energy soon made him a capital farmer; his experiments were so daring that "the simple neighbours who came trembling to ask his advice stood aghast; he, always smiling, gay, affable, having for each a clear, concise counsel, an encouragement enveloped in a pleasantry."

Besides agriculture, his interests extended to banks, railway companies, a manufactory for chemical fertilisers, steam mills for grinding corn, and a line of packets on the Lago Maggiore. During this time he visited England, and was to be seen night after night in the Strangers' Gallery of the House of Commons, making himself master of the methods of parliamentary tactics, that were to be of such value to Italy in later years.

In 1847 Cavour started the *Risorgimento,* a journal whose programme was simply this: "Independence of Italy, union between the princes and peoples, progress in the path of reform, and a league between the Italian states." As for Italian unity, "Let us," Cavour would say, "do one thing at a time; let us get rid of the Austrians, and then—we shall see." After returning from England in 1843 he wrote:

You may well talk to me-of hell, for since I left you I live in a kind of intellectual hell, where intelligence and science are reputed infernal by him who has the goodness to govern us.

The king, Charles Albert, had called him the most dangerous man in the kingdom, and he certainly was the most dangerous to the old systems of religious and political bigotry; but his work was educational; gradually he was enlightening the minds of the masses, and preventing a possible reign of terror. In 1848 he wrote:

> What is it which has always wrecked the finest and justest of revolutions? The mania for revolutionary means; the men who have attempted to emancipate themselves from ordinary laws. Revolutionary means, producing the directory, the consulate, and the empire; Napoleon, bending all to his caprice, imagining that one can with a like facility conquer at the Bridge of Lodi and wipe out a law of nature. Wait but a little longer, and you will see the last consequence of your revolutionary means— Louis Napoleon on the throne!

Charles Albert, the king, who, as Prince Carignan, had been one of the Carbonari, and secretly hated Austria, has been accused of treachery and double dealing (he explained that he was "always between the dagger of the Carbonari and the chocolate of the Jesuits"); but the time came when he nobly redeemed his past. In 1845 he assured d'Azeglio that when Sardinia was ready to free herself from Austria, his life, his sons' lives, his arms, his treasure, should all be freely spent in the Italian cause.

In February, 1848, he granted his people a constitution; a parliament was formed, Cavour becoming member for Turin.

In this month the Revolution broke out in Paris and penetrated to the heart of Vienna. Metternich was forced to fly his country; the Austrians left Milan; Venice threw off the yoke—all Italy revolted. The Pope, it is said, behaved badly, and left Rome free for Garibaldi to enter, with Mazzini enrolled as a volunteer.

Even the abominable Ferdinand of Sicily and the Grand Duke of Tuscany had been obliged to grant constitutions; all the northern states had hastened to unite themselves to Sardinia by universal plebiscite. At the very beginning Charles

Albert fulfilled his pledge; he placed himself at the head of his army and defied Austria.

But it was too soon: Austria was too strong. On the 23rd of March, 1849, Charles Albert was crushingly defeated by Radetsky at Novara. There, when night fell, he called his generals to him, and in their presence abdicated in favour of his son, Victor Emmanuel, who knelt weeping before him. The pathos of despair was in his words: "Since I have not succeeded in finding death," he said, "I must accomplish one last sacrifice for my country."

He left the battle-field and his country without even visiting his home; six months later he was dead. "The magnanimous king," his people called him.

The young Victor Emmanuel began his reign in a kingly fashion; pointing his sword towards the Austrian camp, he exclaimed: *"Per Dio! d'Italia sara."* It seemed at the time a mere empty boast—his little country was brought so close to the verge of ruin. The terms of peace imposed an Austrian occupation until the war indemnity of eighty million francs should be paid. Yet Cavour was heard to say that all their sacrifices were not too dear a price for the Italian tricolour in exchange for the flag of Savoy. It was not until July that Rome fell—Rome, where Garibaldi had established a republic and Mazzini was a Triumvir!

At the invitation of the Pope, Louis Napoleon, then president of the French republic, seeing the opportunity for conciliating the religious powers, poured his troops into Rome, and Garibaldi fled, with Anita at his side. The brave wife with her unborn child would not leave her hero, but death took her from him. In a peasant's hut, a few days later, she died, his arms around her. As for Mazzini, the fall of Rome nearly broke his heart. For days he wandered dazed about the Eternal City, miraculously escaping capture, till his friends got him away.

It was not until April of 1850 that Pius IX. dared to come back to Rome, where a body of French troops long remained, to show how really religious a nation was France. From his accession there had been a papal party in Italy, who, because of the good manners of the gentle ecclesiastic, had wrought themselves up to believe that Italy could be united under *him*. But as early as 1847 d'Azeglio wrote from Rome:

> The magic of Pio Nono will not last; he is an angel, but he is surrounded by demons.

After the events of the 1848 rising, and his appeal (twenty-five pontiffs had made the same appeal before him!) to the foreigner against his own people, the dream of a patriotic pope melted into thin air.

And so Austria came back into Italy, and seemed again complete master there. It would be interesting to be able to analyse the sensibilities of these prince-puppets who were jerked back to their thrones by their master at Vienna. Plenty of Austrian troops came to take care of them. As for the bitter reprisals Italians had to bear, it is almost impossible to read of them. In certain provinces every one found with a weapon was put to death. A man found with a rusty nail was promptly shot. At Brescia a little hunchback was slowly burnt alive. Women, stripped half naked, were flogged in the marketplace, with Austrian officers looking on. It was after his visit to Naples in the winter of 1850 that Gladstone wrote, "This is the negation of God erected into a system of government."

But Italy had now a new champion. When Victor Emmanuel signed his name to the first census in his reign, he jestingly gave his occupation as "Re Galantuomo," and this name stuck to him for ever after. A brave monarch Victor Emmanuel proved, whose courage and honesty were tried in many fires.

When arranging negotiations with Radetsky after Novara, he was given to understand that the conditions of peace would be much more favourable if he would abandon the constitution granted by Charles Albert.

"Marshal," he said, "sooner than subscribe to such conditions, I would lose a hundred crowns. What my father has sworn I will maintain. If you wish a war to the death, be it so! My house knows the road of exile, but not of dishonour."

The Princes of Piedmont had been always renowned for physical courage and dominating minds. Effeminacy and mendacity are not their foibles. It is hinted by the Countess of Cesaresco, in her *Liberation of Italy,* that sainthood was esteemed the privilege strictly of the women of the family; but then sainthood is not absolutely necessary to a monarch. The Piedmont line had always understood the business of kings,—but none so thoroughly as Victor Emmanuel.

He was unpopular at first; the Mazzinists cried, "Better Italy enslaved than handed over to the son of the traitor, Carlo Alberto!" On the wall of his palace at Turin was written: "It is all up with us; we have a German king and queen"—alluding to the Austrian origin of his mother and of his young queen, Marie Adelaide.

These two—wife and mother—were ruled by clerics, and made his life melancholy when he began a course of ecclesiastical reform. One person in every two hundred and fourteen in Sardinia was an ecclesiastic, and the Church had control of all ecclesiastical jurisdiction and could shelter criminals, among other mediaeval privileges. To reform these abuses, the king, in 1849, approached the pope with deferential requests, but the pope absolutely refused to make any changes.

However, the work of reform was firmly pushed on, and a law was passed by which the priestly privileges were sensibly cut down, although the king's wife and mother wrung their hands, and the religious press shrieked denunciation. At this time Santa Rosa, the Minister of Commerce and Agriculture, died, and the Church refused him the last sacrament, though he was a blameless and devout member of the Roman Church. This hateful act of intolerance reacted on the clergy, as a matter of course, and gave an impetus to church reform.

When, in 1855, Victor Emmanuel was so unfortunate as to lose his wife, his mother, and his brother, within a month, and the nation as a whole mourned with him, his clerical friends embittered his affliction by insisting with venomous frankness that it was the judgment of Heaven that he had brought upon himself for his religious persecutions.

Strength was Victor Emmanuel's genius: he was not intellectual in any marked degree, but his ministers could work with him and rely upon him. A union between him and Cavour, the two great men of the kingdom, was inevitable. Up to this time Cavour had no general fame except as a journalist, but the king had the insight to recognise his extraordinary powers, and when Santa Rosa died (unshriven) Cavour in his place became Minister of Agriculture and Commerce. "Look out!" said the king to his prime minister, d'Azeglio, when this had come to pass, "Cavour will soon be taking all your portfolios. He will never rest till he is prime minister himself."

Under the regime of Cavour, railways and telegraph wires lined the kingdom in all directions; he took off foolish tariffs and concluded commercial treaties with England, France, Belgium, and other powers. "Milord Cavour" was a nickname showing the dislike aroused by his English predilections, but through him Piedmont repaired the damage of the war of 1848, and grew steadily in prosperity.

Cavour's brilliant intellectual powers seem to have been so limitless that it is rather a relief to think of him personally" as only a dumpy little man with an over-big head. Although a born aristocrat, and living in the manner becoming one, he was capable of quite demonstrative behaviour. The occasion for this was a dinner given by d'Azeglio. Cavour, seated at table, joked the premier about his jealousy of Ratazzi; the premier replied angrily; whereupon the greatest of diplomats arose, seized his plate, lifting it as high as he could, and dashed it to the floor, where it broke into fragments. Then he rushed out of the house, crying: "He is a beast! He is a beast!" This quarrel, which sounds like an act from a nursery drama, led to a change in the cabinet, with Cavour left out. But a little later on d'Azeglio resigned, and Cavour was prime minister.

A marvellous stroke of statesmanship on behalf of his country was Cavour's intervention in the Crimean War in 1855,— three years after Louis Napoleon's *coup detat*. It seemed an act of folly to send fifteen thousand troops from the little Italian state—which had no standing among European powers—to help England and France. The undertaking seemed to Sardinians an act of insanity; Cavour's colleagues were violently against him. But the king stood by him; so the troops were sent and the ministers resigned.

Never was an action more fully justified. At the close of the Crimean War Sardinia had two powerful allies—France and England; and for the first time she was admitted on terms of equality among the "Powers." A significant thing had been said, too, in 1855: "What can I do for Italy?" asked the Emperor Napoleon of Cavour. Cavour was not slow to tell him what could be done; he was convinced that he must look for aid to the vanity and ambition of Napoleon III.

No diplomatic pressure of his, however, availed. During the next two years the attitude of Austria became constantly more unendurable, but still Napoleon would make no move.

It proved to be the most unlikely of events that brought about a consummation of the wishes of Cavour.

On the evening of January 14, 1858, a carriage drove through the Paris streets on its way to the opera. With the appearance of its two occupants all the world is familiar; the wonderful Spanish eyes of the lady, the exquisite lines of her figure—who has not seen them pictured? The smallish man with her had been described by the Crown Prince of Prussia as having "strangely immobile features and almost extinguished eyes." His huge moustache had exaggeratedly long waxed ends, and his chin was covered with an "imperial."

The terrible crash of Orsini's bombs, thrown underneath their carriage, failed to carry out the conspirators' purpose. The emperor had a slight wound on the nose, and the empress felt a blow on the eye. That was all, except that her silks and laces were spattered with blood from the wounded outside the carriage. They continued their drive and saw the opera to its finish before they were told of the tragedy that had befallen. Eight people had been killed and one hundred and fifty-six wounded by the explosion.

The Empress Eugenie, it is said, showed the greatest composure over the event, but this was not true of her husband. Probably no man of modern times had had so many attempts made on his life as Louis Napoleon, and always, before, he made light of them; but this last one, resulting in such cruel slaughter, completely unnerved him. He now lived in a tremor, dreading the vengeance of still others of the revolutionary ex-friends of his youth; but he dared not relax the despotic grip with which he ruled his land. How could he placate them? He wore a cuirass under his coat; he had wires netted over the chimneys of the Tuileries, so that bombs should not burst on his hearth; a swarm of detectives were around him wherever he went, and always the question asked itself in his mind: What should he do to take off the curse of fear from his life?

Cavour, Victor Emmanuel, the whole of Italy, were filled with rage and disgust at the news of Orsini's attempt. Orsini—an Italian! That must be the end of all their hopes of help from France! But in the summer of 1848 Cavour was summoned to the emperor at Plombieres, and during two days there the agreement was formulated by which France and Italy united against Austria. This was Louis Napoleon's solution of his problem—to help Italy at least sufficiently to annul the hate of every assassin on the peninsula. According to the Prince Regent of Prussia, he chose *la guerre* instead of *le poignard*.

No written record was made of the bargain between Napoleon and Cavour; but we know that it gave Savoy and Nice to France, and made one innocent royal victim, the young Princess Clotilde, Victor Emmanuel's daughter, who was there betrothed by proxy to Prince Jerome Napoleon.

It was at Plombieres that Napoleon with some naiveté said to Cavour: "Do you know, there are but three *men* in all Europe: one is myself, the second is you, and the third is one whose name I will not mention." Napoleon was not alone in his high estimate of Cavour. In Turin they said: "We have a ministry, a parliament, a constitution; all *that* spells Cavour."

At his reception on New Year's Day, 1859, Napoleon astounded every one by greeting the Austrian ambassador with these words: "I regret that our relations with your government are not so good as they have been hitherto." This ostentatious expression was equal to publication in a journal. Immediate war was looked for by every one. Piedmont, France, and Austria openly made bellicose preparations.

Although on the 18th of January, 1859, a formal treaty was made, by which France was bound to support Piedmont if attacked by Austria, Napoleon hesitated and tried to back out of his agreement. It will never be known by what tortuous system of diplomacy Cavour compelled Austria herself to declare war, but it was done, April 27.

Cavour's intrigues during these days were dazzlingly complicated; he had to deal on one hand with his imperial ally, and on the other with shady revolutionary elements—and to keep his right hand in ignorance of what his left hand did. He summoned Garibaldi to Turin; Garibaldi, in his loose red shirt and sombrero, with its plume, with his tumultuous hair and beard, struck dismay to the heart of the servant who opened the door. He refused to admit him, but finally agreed to consult his master. "Let him come in," said Cavour. "It is probably some poor devil who has a petition to make to me." This was the first meeting of the statesman and the warrior. When told of the French alliance, Garibaldi exclaimed: "Mind what you are about! Never forget that the aid of foreign armies must be, in some way or other, dearly paid for!" But his adherence was whole-heartedly given to Victor Emmanuel, and at the end of the short campaign Italy rang with his name.

For months past Austria had been pouring troops into Italy—there seemed no limit to them. Garibaldi, by the end of April, was in command of a band of Cacciatori delli Alpi, a small force, but made up of the iron men of North Italy, worthy of their leader.

On May 2 Victor Emmanuel took the command of his army; it comprised fifty-six thousand infantry in five divisions, one division of cavalry in sixteen squadrons, with twelve field-guns and two batteries of horse artillery. On May 12 the French emperor rode through the streets of Genoa amid loud acclamations; the city was hung with draperies and garlands in his honour. At Alessandria he rode under an arch on which was inscribed, "To the descendant of the Conqueror of Marengo!" In all he had one hundred and twenty-eight thousand men, including ten thousand cavalry.

It was a short campaign, but the weeks were thick with battles, and the battlefields with the slain.

The first engagement was at Genestrello, May 20. The Austrians, driven out, made a stand at Montebello, where, though twenty thousand strong, they were routed by six thousand Sardinians. The armies of the emperor and king forced the Austrians to cross the Po, and there retire behind the Sesia. On the 30th the allies crossed the Sesia and drove the foe from the fortified positions of Palestro, Venzaglio, and Casalino.

Next came Magenta—a splendid triumph for MacMahon; the Austrian loss was ten thousand men; that of the French between four thousand and five thousand. Meantime, Garibaldi had led his Cacciatori to the Lombard shores of Lake Maggiore, had beaten the Austrians at Varese, entered Como, routed the enemy again at San Fermo, and was now proceeding to Bergamo and Brescia with the purpose of cutting off the enemy's retreat through the Alps of the Trentino.

On the 8th of June Victor Emmanuel and Napoleon III. made their triumphal entry into Milan, from whence every Austrian had fled. Every one remembers how MacMahon, now Duke of Magenta, caught up to his saddle-bow a child who was in danger of being crushed by the crowd.

The emperor and the king soon moved on from Milan. By the 23rd their headquarters were fixed at Montechiaro, close to the site of the coming battle of Solferino.

On the day before the battle the lines of the allies lay near the Austrian lines, from the shore of the Lake of Garda at San Martino to Cavriana on the extreme right. On the evening of the 23rd there was issued a general order regulating the movements of the allied forces: Victor Emmanuel's army was sent to the extreme left, near Lake Garda; Baraguay d'Hilliers was given the centre in front of Solferino, which was the Austrian centre; to his right was MacMahon, next Marshal Niel, and then Canrobert at the extreme right, while the emperor's guards were ordered here and there in the changes of the battle.

The enemy, under Field-Marshal Stadion, held the entire line of battle strongly, with one hundred and forty thousand men.

Solferino has been the scene of many combats; it is a natural fighting-ground, and the Austrians had barricaded themselves at all the strong points of vantage.

At five in the morning of the 24th, Louis Napoleon sat in his shirt-sleeves, after his early coffee, smoking a cigar, when tidings came to him that the fighting had begun. In a few minutes he was driving at full speed to Castiglione, and on the way he said to an aide: "The fate of Italy is perhaps to be decided to-day." It was he indeed who decided it; whatever else is said of him, it was he who struck a great blow for Italy at Solferino.

It was the great day of Napoleon III.; he has never been considered a notable soldier, but throughout this day, in every command issued, he displayed consummate military ability.

The sun glared in the intense blue above with tropical heat, when, at Castiglione, Napoleon climbed the steeple of St. Peter's Church and beheld the expanse of Lake Garda, growing dim towards the Tyrolean Alps. There was the remnant of an ancient castle—a sturdy tower—guarding the village of Solferino, called the "Spy of Italy." Already a deadly fire from its loopholes poured on Baraguay d'Hilliers's men, who faced it bravely, but were falling in terrible numbers.

He could see the Austrian masses swarming along the heights uniting Cavriana with Solferino. The Piedmontese cannon booming from the left told that Victor Emmanuel was fighting hard, but his forces were hidden by hills. It was at once plain to him, from his church steeple, that the object of the Austrians was to divert the attack on Solferino—the key of their position—by outflanking the French right, filling up the gap between the Second and Fourth Corps, and thus cutting the emperor's army in two. Coming down from his height, Napoleon at once sent orders to the cavalry of the Imperial Guard to join MacMahon, to prevent his forces from being divided. Altogether the emperor's plan seems to have been clear and definite; his design was to carry Solferino at any cost, and then, by a flank movement, to beat the enemy out of his positions at Cavriana. Galloping to the top of Monte Fenil, the emperor beheld a thick phalanx of bayonets thrust its way suddenly through the trees of the valley; it was a huge body of Austrians sent to cut off the line of the French. There was not a minute to be lost; he sent orders to General Maneque, of the Guard, to advance at once against the Austrian columns. With magnificent rapidity the order was executed, and the Austrians—a great number—were beaten back far from the line of battle.

The Austrian batteries placed on the Mount of Cypresses

and on the Cemetery Hill of Solferino were keeping up a deadly fire on the French.

Baraguay d'Hilliers brought Bazaine's brigade into action against the one, and the First Regiment of zouaves rushed up the other, only to be hurled back by the enemy as they reached the steep slope. A horrible confusion followed these two repulses, the zouaves and General Negrier's division being fatally mixed and fighting with each other like furies. But General Negrier kept his head and collected his troops, scattered all over the hillocks and valleys. Then, with the Sixty-first Regiment of the line and a battalion of the One Hundredth Regiment, he started resolutely to mount the Cemetery Hill. It was a deadly march; the enemy, holding the advantage, disputed every turn and twist of the ascent. Twice Negrier's troops rushed up along the ridge-like path, but the circular wall of the cemetery, bored with thousands of holes, through which rifles sent a scathing hail, was strong as a fortress to resist them. It was sheer murder to take his men up again; Negrier" abandoned the attack.

The enemy's cannon-balls from the three defended heights fell thick and fast on Mount Fenil, where Napoleon and his aides breathlessly watched the progress of the drama.

Many of the Cent-Gardes who formed the imperial escort were shot down; the emperor was in the midst of death. The Austrians had been strongly reinforced, and held to the defence of Solferino more obstinately than ever.

But, notwithstanding this, the French were gaining ground; the left flank of the Austrians was at last broken by the artillery of the French reserve, and the whole army felt a thrill of encouragement.

A number of French battalions were now massing themselves about the spur of the Tower Hill of Solferino, but it was impossible to proceed to the attack while solid Austrian masses stood ready to pounce upon their flank.

A few fiery charges scattered the enemy in all directions,

and-a tempest of shouts rang out when Forey gave the order to storm the Tower Hill. The drum beat, the trumpets sounded. *"Vive l'Empereur!"* echoed from the encircling hills. *Quick* is too slow a word for French soldiers. The Imperial Guard, chasseurs, and battalions of the line rushed up with such fierce velocity that it was no time at all before the heights of Solferino were covered with Napoleon's men. Nothing could stand against such an electric shock—the Tower Hill was carried, and General Leboeuf turned the artillery on the defeated masses of Austrians choking up the road that led to Cavriana.

The convent and adjoining church, strongly barricaded, yielded after repeated attacks, and then Baraguay d'Hilliers and Negrier made a last attempt on the Cemetery Hill. The narrow path that led up to it was strewn with bloody corpses, but neither the dead resting in their graves nor these new dead could be held sacred. A strong artillery fire on the gate and walls stopped the rifles from firing through the holes, and in this pause Colonel Laffaile led the Seventy-eighth Regiment up. They burst in the gate of the cemetery,— there were not many there to kill!—they were soon on their way towards the village.

Their way lay through a checker-board of tiny farms and fields, separated by stone walls wreathed with ivy. Little chapels, dedicated to favourite saints, stood in every enclosure. Houses, walls, and chapels had all been turned into barricades by the Austrians. Douay's and Negrier's men had to fight their way to the village through a rain of bullets from unseen enemies. Now they took the narrow path winding up by the Tower Hill into the streets of the village; when nearly at the top the clanking of heavy artillery-wheels told them that the enemy were retreating and carrying off the very guns that had played such havoc on their ranks from the top of Tower Hill. It took but a short time to capture them, and then they were fairly in the village, chasing the last straggling Austrians through the streets.

Solferino was in the hands of the French; but the fate of the battle was not yet decided, for Cavriana was a strong position, and Stadion and his generals had made a careful study of its possibilities.

At two o'clock MacMahon's left wing was completely surrounded by the enemy, but moving forward on the right he boldly turned the Austrian front, and swept everything before him to the village of San Cassiano, adjoining Cavriana. The village was attacked on both sides and carried by Laure's Algerian sharpshooters; but the Austrians still held Monte Fontana, which unites San Cassiano to Cavriana, and repulsed Laure's men with deadly skill.

Reinforced, they made a splendid dash and took Monte Fontana, but the Prince of Hesse brought up reserves and won it back for the Austrians. Napoleon now ordered Mac-Mahon to push forward his whole corps to support the attack, and as Maneque's brigade and Mellinet's grenadiers had succeeded in routing the enemy from Monte Sacro, they were ordered to advance on Cavriana.

Lebœuf placed the artillery of the Guard at the opening of the valley facing Cavriana, and Laure's Algerian sharpshooters after a prolonged hand-to-hand conflict with the Prince of Hesse's men carried Cavriana at four o'clock. Two hours later Napoleon was resting in the Casa Pastore, where the Austrian emperor had slept the night before. The sultry glare of the day had culminated in a wild, black storm; the wind was a hurricane, and it was under torrents of rain that the Austrians made their retreat, while the thunder drowned the noise of Marshal Neil's cannon driving them from every stand they made.

Such overwhelming numbers had been brought to bear on the French that day that their, defeat would have been almost certain if it had not been for Napoleon's generalship and his modern rifled guns. These were new to the Austrians, who became panic-stricken at their effect.

The Piedmontese troops, under their "Re Galantuomo," fought as nobly as their brilliant allies that day. The young Emperor Francis Joseph commanded in person at San Martino, but it was Benedek that Victor Emmanuel had to reckon with—the best general of all the Austrian staff. He beat him out of San Martino, and to the Italians the combat of June 24 is known as the Battle of San Martino to this day.

The scorching sun of next morning shone upon twenty-two thousand ghastly dead. It has been believed that the horrible sights and scents of this battlefield sickened the emperor and cut short the campaign; but who can tell? Was it perhaps Eugenie's influence—always used in favour of the pope? Or was it that he realised that the movement could now only end in the complete liberation of Italy—a consummation that he regarded with horror? All that is known is this: three days after the Austrians had been driven back to their own country, and while all Italy went mad with joy at the victory, while Mrs. Browning was writing her *Emperor Evermore*—a cruel satire on later events—it became known that Napoleon had sent a message to the Austrian Kaiser asking him to suspend hostilities.

The two emperors met at Villafranca, a small place near Solferino. At the close of their interview Francis Joseph looked humiliated and sombre—Louis Napoleon was smilingly at ease. He, the parvenu, had made terms with a legitimate emperor, and was pleased with himself. He had arranged that Lombardy was to be united to Piedmont, while Venetia remained Austrian. When Victor Emmanuel was told of these terms he could only say coldly that he must ever remain grateful for what Napoleon *had* done, but he murmured "Poor Italy!"

And Cavour? Cavour was struck to the heart. Had he arranged such a finale as *this* with the upstart emperor—that he should leave the game when it suited his pleasure, and make terms with the Austrian emperor all by himself—insolently disregarding Victor Emmanuel? He wept with grief and anger. He left at once for the camp, and there he told the emperor his opinion of him in stinging words. He begged his king to repudiate the treaty and reject Lombardy, but Victor Emmanuel, although as bitterly disappointed as Cavour, felt that he must be prudent for his people's sake.

Angered at the king's refusal, Cavour resigned his office and retired to his farms at Leri, but after a few months he was back in his old place in the cabinet. All his hopes and ambitions came back—although physically the shock had broken him—and he laboured for Italy till his death in June of 1861. The whole Italian people, from king to peasant, knew that they had lost their best friend. But Cavour's life-work was nearly finished. Garibaldi had taken up the work of emancipation where Napoleon had abandoned it, and before he left him for ever, to Cavour was given the triumph of hearing his beloved master proclaimed King of Italy.

The Battle of
Bunker Hill

AT THE FENCE——THE BATTLE OF BUNKER HILL

The Battle of Bunker Hill

On the 12th of June, 1775, Captain Harris, afterwards Lord Harris, wrote home from the town of Boston, then occupied by British troops:

> I wish the Americans may be brought to a sense of their duty. One good drubbing, which I long to give them, by way of retaliation, might have a good effect towards it. At present they are so elated by the petty advantage they gained the 19th of April, that they despise the powers of Britain. We shall soon take the field on the other side of the Neck.

This very fairly expressed the irritation in the British camp. The troops had been sent to Massachusetts to subdue it, but as yet nothing had been done in that direction.

The ignominious flight of the British regulars from Lexington and Concord was still unavenged. More than that, they had been kept close in Boston ever since by the provincial militia.

"What!" cried General Burgoyne when on his arrival in May he was told this news. "What! Ten thousand peasants keep five thousand King's troops shut up? Let *us* get in, and we'll soon find elbow-room! "*Elbow-room* was the army's name for Burgoyne after that.

A little later General Gage remarked to General Timothy Ruggles, "It is impossible for the rebels to withstand our arms a moment."

Ruggles replied: "Sir, you do not know with whom you have to contend. These are the very men who conquered Canada. I fought with them side by side. I know them well; they will fight bravely. My God, sir, your folly has ruined your cause!"

Besides Burgoyne, the *Cerberus* brought over Generals Clinton and Howe, and large reinforcements, so that the forces under General Gage, the commander-in-chief, were over ten thousand. By June 12 the army in Boston was actually unable to procure fresh provisions, and Gage proclaimed martial law, designating those who were in arms as rebels and traitors.

The *Essex Gazette* of June 8 says: We have the pleasure to inform the public that the Grand American Army is nearly completed." This Grand American Army was spread around Boston, its headquarters at Cambridge, under command of General Artemas Ward, who had fought under Abercromby. The Grand American Army was an army of allies. Ward, its supposed chief, was authorised to command only the Massachusetts and New Hampshire forces, and when the Connecticut and Rhode Island men obeyed him it was purely through courtesy. Each colony supplied its own troops with provisions and ammunition; each had its own officers, appointed by the Committee of Safety.

To this committee, June 13, came the tidings that Gage proposed to occupy Bunker Hill, in Charlestown, on the 18th, and a council of war was held, which included the savagely bluff, warm-hearted patriot, General Israel Putnam, of the Connecticut troops; General Seth Pomeroy; Colonel William Prescott; the hardy, independent Stark; and Captain Gridley, the engineer—all of whom were veterans of the French and Indian war.

As a result of the meeting, a detachment of nine hundred men of the Massachusetts regiments, under Colonels Prescott, Frye, and Bridge, with two hundred men from Connecticut, and Captain Grid-ley's artillery company of forty-nine men and two field-pieces, were ordered to parade at six o'clock p.m., the 16th, on Cambridge Common. There they appeared with weapons, packs, blankets, and entrenching tools. President Langdon, of Harvard College, made an impressive prayer, and by nine o'clock they had marched, the entire force being under the command of Colonel Prescott.

A uniform of blue turned back with red was worn by some of the men, but for the most part they wore their "Sunday suits" of homespun. Their guns were of all sorts and sizes, and many carried old-fashioned powder-horns and pouches. Prescott walked at their head, with two sergeants carrying dark lanterns, until they; reached the Neck.

The Neck was the strip of land leading to the peninsula opposite Boston, where lay the small town of Charlestown. The peninsula is only one mile in length, its greatest breadth but half a mile. The Charles River separates it from Boston on the south, and to the north and east is the Mystic River. Bunker Hill begins at the isthmus and rises gradually to a height of one hundred and ten feet, forming a smooth round hill.

At Cambridge Common, the night the troops started for Bunker Hill, Israel Putnam had made this eloquent address: "Men, there are enough of you on the Common this evening to fill hell so full of the redcoats to-morrow that the devils will break their shins over them."

At Bunker Hill the expedition halted, and a long discussion ensued between Prescott, Gridley, Major Brooks, and Putnam as to whether it would be better to follow Ward's orders literally and fortify Bunker Hill itself, or to go on to the lesser elevation south-east of it, which is now known as Breed's Hill, but had then no special name. They agreed upon Breed's Hill. They began to entrench at midnight.

Prescott was consumed with anxiety lest his men should be attacked before some screen could be raised to shelter them. However enthusiastic they might be, he did not think it possible for his raw troops to meet to any advantage a disciplined soldiery in the open field.

So the pickaxe and the spade were busy throughout the night. It was silent work, for the foe was near. In Boston Harbour lay the *Lively,* the *Somerset,* the *Cerberus,* the *Glasgow,* the *Falcon,* and the *Symmetry,* besides the floating batteries. On the Boston shore the sentinels were pacing outside the British encampment. At intervals through the night Prescott and Brooks stole down to the shore of Charles River and listened till the call of "All's well!" rang over the water from the ships and told them that their scheme was still undiscovered.

At dawn the entrenchments were six feet high, and there was a great burst of fire at them from the *Lively,* which was joined in a few moments by the other men-of-war and the batteries on Copp's Hill, on the Boston shore.

The strange thunder of the cannonade brought forth every man, woman, and child in Boston. Out of their prim houses they rushed under trellises heavy with damask roses and honeysuckle, and soon every belfry and tower, house-top and hill-top, was crowded with them. There the most of them stayed till the thrilling play in which they had so vital an interest was enacted.

Meanwhile Prescott, to inspire his raw men with confidence, mounted the parapet of the redoubt they had raised, and deliberately sauntered around it, making jocular speeches, until the men cheered each cannon-ball as it came.

Gage, looking through his field-glasses from the other shore, marked the tall figure with the three-cornered hat and the banyan—a linen blouse—buckled about the waist, and asked of Councillor Willard, who stood near him: "Who is the person who appears to command? "

"That is my brother-in-law, Colonel Prescott."

"Will he fight?"

"Yes, sir; he is an old soldier, and will fight as long as a drop of blood remains in his veins."

"The works must be carried," said Gage.

Gage was strongly advised by his generals to land a force

at the Neck and attack the Americans in the rear. It was also suggested that they might be bombarded by the fleet from the Mystic and the Charles, and, indeed, might be starved out without any fighting at all. But none of this suited the warlike British temper; the whole army longed to fight—to chase the impudent enemy out of those entrenchments he had so insolently reared. The challenge was a bold one; it must be accepted. The British had the weight in all ways, but they also had the preposterous arrogance of the British army, which always deems itself invincible because it remembers its traditions, and traditions are dubious and improper weapons to fire at a foe.

At noon the watchers on the house-tops saw the lines of smart grenadiers and light infantry embark in barges under command of General Howe, who had with him Brigadier-General Pigot and some of the most distinguished officers in Boston. They landed at the south-western point of the peninsula.

When the intelligence that the British troops had landed reached Cambridge it caused great excitement. A letter of Captain Chester reads:

Just after dinner on the 17th ult. I was walking out from my lodgings, quite calm and composed, and all at once the drums beat to arms, and bells rang, and a great noise in Cambridge. Captain Putnam came by on full gallop. 'What is the matter?' says I. 'Have you not heard?' 'No.' 'Why, the regulars are landing at Charlestown,' says he, 'and father says you must all meet and march immediately to Bunker Hill to oppose the enemy.' I waited not, but ran and got my arms and ammunition, and hastened to my company (who were in the church for barracks), and found them nearly ready to march. We soon marched, with our frocks and trousers on over our other clothes (for our company is in uniform wholly blue, turned up with red), for we were loath to expose ourselves by our dress; and down we marched."

After a reconnaissance, Howe sent back to Gage for reinforcements, and remained passive until they came.

Meanwhile, there were bitter murmurings among the troops on Breed's Hill. They had watched the brilliant pageant,—the crossing over of their adversaries, scarlet-clad, with glittering equipments, with formidable guns in their train,— and were conscious of being themselves exhausted from the night's labour and the hot morning sun. It was two o'clock, and they had had practically nothing to eat that day. Among themselves they accused their officers of treachery. It seemed incredible that after doing all the hard work they should be expected to do the fighting as well. Loud huzzas arose from their lips, however,—these cross and hungry Yankees,—when Doctor—or General—Joseph Warren appeared among them with Seth Pomeroy.

Few men had risen to a higher degree of universal love and confidence in the hearts of the Massachusetts people than Warren. He had been active in every patriotic movement. The councils through which the machinery of the Revolution was put in motion owed much to him. He was president of the Committee of Safety, and probably had been one of the Indians of the Boston Tea Party. But a few days before he had been appointed major-general. In recognition of this, Israel Putnam, who was keeping a squad of men working at entrenchments on Bunker Hill, had offered to take orders from him. But Warren refused, and asked where he might go to be of the greatest service. "Where will the onset be most furious? "he asked, and Putnam sent him to the redoubt. There Prescott also offered him the chief command, but Warren replied, "I came as a volunteer with my musket to serve under you, and shall be happy to learn from a soldier of your experience."

At three o'clock the redoubt was in good working order. About eight yards square, its strongest side, the front, faced the settled part of Charlestown and protected the south side of the hill. The east side commanded a field; the north side had an open passage-way; to the left extended a breastwork for about two hundred yards.

By three o'clock some reinforcements for General Howe had arrived, so that he now had over three thousand men. Just before action he addressed the officers around him as follows:

"Gentlemen, I am very happy in having the honour of commanding so fine a body of men. I do not in the least doubt that you will behave like Englishmen and as becomes good soldiers. If the enemy will not come out from their entrenchments, we must drive them out at all events; otherwise the town of Boston will be set on fire by them. I shall not desire one of you to go a step farther than where I go myself at your head. Remember, gentlemen, we have no recourse to any resources if we lose Boston but to go on board our ships, which will be very disagreeable to us all."

From the movements of the British, they seemed intending to turn the American left and surround the redoubt. To prevent this, Prescott sent down the artillery with two field-pieces—he had only four altogether—and the Connecticut troops under Captain Knowlton. Putnam met them as they neared the Mystic, shouting—"Man the rail fence, for the enemy is flanking of us fast!"

This rail fence, half of which was stone, reached from the shore of the Mystic to within 200 yards of the breastworks. It was not high, but Putnam had said: "If you can shield a Yankee's shins he's not afraid of anything. His head he does not think of."

Captain Knowlton, joined by Colonels Stark and Reid and their regiments, made another parallel fence a short distance in front of this, filling in the space between with new-mown hay from the fields.

A great cannonade was thundering from ships and batteries to cover Howe's advance. His troops, now increased to three thousand, came on in two divisions: the left wing, under Pigot, towards the breastwork and redoubt; the right, led by Howe, to storm the rail fence. The artillery moved heavily through the miry low ground, and the embarrassing discovery was made that there were only twelve-pound balls for six-pounders. Howe decided to load them with grape. The troops were hindered by. a number of fences, as well as the thick, tall grass. Their knapsacks were extraordinarily heavy, and they felt the power of the scorching sun.

Inside the redoubt the Americans waited for them, Prescott assuring his men that the redcoats would never reach the redoubt if they obeyed him and reserved their fire until he gave the word. As the assaulting force drew temptingly near, the American officers only restrained their men from firing by mounting the parapet and kicking up their guns.

But at last the word was given—the stream of fire broke out all along the line. They were wonderful marksmen. The magnificent regulars were staggered, but they returned the fire. They could make no headway against the murderous volleys flashed in quick succession at them. The dead and wounded fell thickly. General Pigot ordered a retreat, while great shouts of triumph arose from the Americans.

At the rail fence Putnam gave his last directions when Howe was nearing him: "Fire low: aim at the waistbands! Wait until you see the whites of their eyes! Aim at the handsome coats! Pick off the commanders!"

The men rested their guns on the rail fence to fire. The officers were used as targets—many of the handsome coats were laid low. So hot was the reception they met that in a few moments Howe's men were obliged to fall back. One of them said afterwards, "It was the strongest post that was ever occupied by any set of men."

There was wild exultation within the American lines, congratulation and praises, for just fifteen minutes; and then Pigot and Howe led the attack again. But the second repulse was so much fiercer than the first that the British broke ranks and ran down hill, some of them getting into the boats.

"The dead," said Stark, "lay in front of us as thick as sheep in a fold."

Meantime Charlestown had been set on fire by Howe's orders, and the spectacle was splendidly terrible to the watchers in Boston. The wooden buildings made a superb blaze, and through the smoke could be seen the British officers striking and pricking their men with their swords in the vain hope of rallying them, while cannon, musketry, crashes of falling houses, and the yells of the victors filled up the measure of excitement to the spectators.

Twice, now, the Americans had met the foe and proved that he was not invincible. The women in Boston thought the last defeat final—that their men-folk had gained the day. But Prescott knew better; he was sure that they would come again, and sure that he could not withstand a third attack.

If at this juncture strong reinforcements and supplies of ammunition had reached him, he might well have held his own. But such companies as had been sent on would come no farther than Bunker Hill, in spite of Israel Putnam's threats and entreaties. There they straggled about under haycocks and apple-trees, demoralised by the sights and sounds of battle, with no authorised leader who could force them to the front.

As for their commander-in-chief, Ward, he would not stir from his house all day, and kept the main body of his forces at Cambridge.

When General Clinton saw the rout of his countrymen from the Boston shore, he rowed over in great haste. With his assistance, and the fine discipline which prevailed, the troops were re-formed within half an hour. Clinton also proposed a new plan of assault. Accordingly, instead of diffusing their forces across the whole American front, the chief attack was directed on the redoubt. The artillery bombarded the breast-work, and only a small number moved against the rail fence.

"Fight! conquer or die!" was the watchword that passed from mouth to mouth as the tall, commanding figure of Howe led on the third assault. To his soldiers it was a desperate venture—they felt that they were going to certain death. But inside the redoubt few of the men had more than one round of ammunition left, though they shouted bravely:

"We are ready for the redcoats again!". Again their first fire was furious and destructive, but although many of the enemy fell, the rest bounded forward without returning it. In a few minutes the columns of Pigot and Clinton had surrounded the redoubt on three sides. The defenders of the breastwork had been driven by the artillery fire into the redoubt, and balls came whistling through the open passage.

The first rank of redcoats who climbed the parapet was shot down. Major Pitcairn met his death at this time while cheering on his men. But the Americans had come to the end of their ammunition, and they had not fifty bayonets among them, though these were made to do good service as the enemy came swarming over the walls.

Pigot got up by the aid of a tree, and hundreds followed his lead. The Americans made stout resistance in the hand-to-hand struggle that followed, but there could be only one ending to it, and Prescott ordered a retreat. He was almost the last to leave, and only got away by skilfully parrying with his sword the bayonet thrusts of the foe. His banyan was pierced in many places, but he escaped unhurt.

The men at the rail fence kept firm until they saw the forces leaving the redoubt; they fell back then, but in good order. A great volley was fired after the Americans. It was then that Warren fell, as he lingered in the rear—a loss that was passionately mourned throughout New England.

During their disordered flight over the little peninsula the Americans lost more men than at any other time of the day, though their list of killed and wounded only amounted to four hundred and forty-nine. The heavy loss of the enemy—ten hundred and fifty-four men—had the effect of checking the eagerness of their pursuit; the Americans passed the Neck without further molestation.

General Howe had maintained his reputation for solid courage, and his long white silk stockings were soaked in blood.

The speech of Count Vergennes, that "if it won two more such victories as Bunker Hill, there would be no more British Army in America," echoed the general sentiment in England and America as well as in France. So impressed were the British leaders with the indomitable resolution shown by the Provincials in fortifying and defending so desperate a position as Breed's Hill, that they made no attempt to follow up their victory. General Gage admitted that the people of New England were not the despicable rabble they had sometimes been represented.

Among the Grand Army itself many recriminations and courts-martial followed the contest. But Washington soon drilled it into order.

The most important thing to be remembered of Bunker Hill is its effect upon the colonies. The troubles with the mother country had been brewing a long time, but this was the first decisive struggle for supremacy. There was no doubt of the tough, soldierly qualities displayed by the Colonials; the thrill of pride that went through the country at the success of their arms welded together the scattered colonies and made a nation of them. The Revolution was an accomplished fact.

"England," said Franklin, "has lost her colonies for ever."